# Sugar Dough Magic

## FUN CAKES FOR ALL AGES

*Maisie Parrish*

dutton

PUBLISHING

# Foreword

This delightful book is going to produce a great deal of happiness: not only for those of us who are crazy enough to enjoy spending many hours fiddling about with tiny bits of sugar dough, but for the lucky children - and adults - who will be presented with these beautiful and extraordinary edible works of art.

Modelling and covering cakes with sugar dough is enormous fun, and Maisie explains carefully and sympathetically just how she achieves her effects, so that the book will be an inspiration for both the beginner and the more experienced decorator. The clearly illustrated step by step instructions will help even the most anxious newcomer to have a go, and I particularly like the sections on body modelling: from head to toe (including those vital facial expressions) everything is made simple.

I've been a fan of Maisie's for some time, and in this collection she's really surpassed herself. The range of designs is terrific, and I've struggled to pick a favourite (although I must admit my girlie side is very stirred by the gorgeous ballerinas on page 72, and who could resist those exhausted-looking lambs on page 26. Have a look through these pages and marvel: and then make a little magic yourself.

*To Lucy Maisie, my special angel - Popar, and my daughter, Sheree, for her love and encouragement.*

# Acknowledgements

Special thanks to: my husband, Russell, for getting me everywhere on time; Mick Foley of Puppetoon Productions for his steadfast belief and support; Siriol Productions for opening my eyes to the wonderful world of animation; and Beverley, Sue Hodges, Sarah and Jenny for making all things possible.

First published in October 2002 by B. Dutton Publishing Limited, The Grange, Hones Yard, Farnham, Surrey, GU9 8BB.

Reprinted in September 2010 and December 2012.

Copyright: Maisie Parrish 2002

ISBN-10: 0-9532588-4-X

ISBN-13: 978-0-9532588-4-0

Publisher: Beverley Dutton

Editor: Jenny Stewart

Design: Sarah Richardson

Photography: Alister Thorpe

Printed in China

# Introduction

My career in craft modelling began with salt dough. Because there were no books available to help me at the time, I became completely self-taught, working everything out for myself to create a style of my own.

Once I was invited to design something in Sugar Dough, I was really in my element - it was so convenient, trouble-free and easy to use, and everything looked so much prettier.

Every project I make always has its own unique story to tell. I often find that there is so much going on around the cake it is difficult to tell the front from the back! So, you see, I gain so much pleasure from my work I just get carried away.

Once you have mastered the art of figure modelling in sugar, you will find that you can create a cake based around almost any subject and you can make and dress the figures to look just the way you want them to. Of course, I must warn you that it becomes very addictive! Once you get started, you will discover an endless array of 'must have' cutters and tools, and you will no doubt acquire many boxes with lots of small compartments to keep them safe. Above all, you will never lose the desire to learn more.

This book is a legacy of thirteen years of dedication to my craft. My dearest wish is that you too will find plenty to inspire you within its pages and weave some of your own Sugar Dough Magic!

Enjoy,

*Maisie*

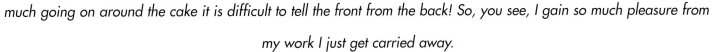

# Contents

Working with Sugar Dough . . . . . . . . . . . . . . . . . . . . 8-10

Techniques . . . . . . . . . . . . . . . . . . . . . . . . . . . . . . . . . 11-12

Essential Tools for Modelling . . . . . . . . . . . . . . . . . . 13

Figure Modelling . . . . . . . . . . . . . . . . . . . . . . . . . . . . 14-18

Dressing Figures . . . . . . . . . . . . . . . . . . . . . . . . . . . . 18-20

Hints and Tips . . . . . . . . . . . . . . . . . . . . . . . . . . . . . 20

Conversion Tables . . . . . . . . . . . . . . . . . . . . . . . . . . 21

22-25
Let's Party

36-41
The Uninvited Guests

26-30
A Day in the Country

42-49
Grandma's Garden

31-35
Victorian Toy Box

50-52
Dish of the Day

53-57
Faithful Friends

58-62
Piggy Plonk

63-71
Gone Fishin'

72-75
Dance Ballerina, Dance!

76-83
Serendipity in the Wild

84-88
Ducks Keep Out!

89-95
Santa's Grotto

96-103
Away with the Fairies

104-108
Just Married

Templates . . . . . . . . . . . . . . .109-111
Stockists . . . . . . . . . . . . . . .112

# Working with Sugar Dough
## What is Sugar Dough?

Sugar Dough is an edible medium which is ideal for modelling, including figure modelling, and can also be used as a cake covering. It is available in eleven different colours.

The main advantages of Sugar Dough are its ease of use, convenience as a ready-coloured medium and, though it will firm as it dries, it will stay soft enough to eat. It can also be coloured with paste and dust colours.

Sugar Dough will fulfill most tasks very well without the need to add anything to it. However, there are two instances where you may wish to do so:

• When extruding paste through a sugar shaper, the paste must be soft in consistency. Knead a little white vegetable fat into the paste before pushing it through the shaper.

• If you are making something that is a supportive piece and therefore requires a little bit of extra strength, add a little gum tragacanth to the paste.

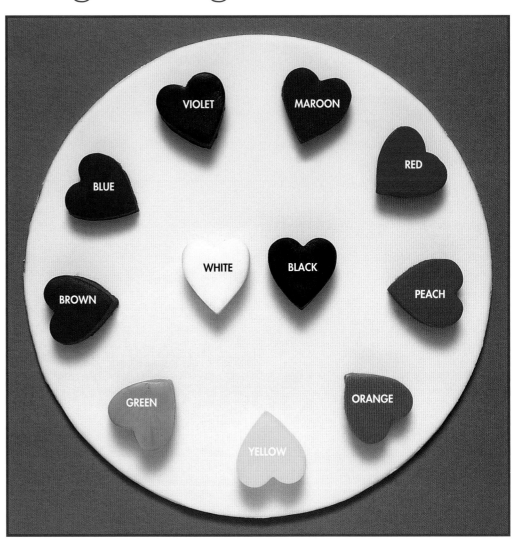

## Storing Sugar Dough

Once you have opened a packet of Sugar Dough, it is important to keep any remaining paste airtight. Rather than leaving it exposed to the air where it will dry out, rub a little white vegetable fat over your hands and knead the paste until it is soft and pliable. Roll it into a thick sausage shape and wrap it up tightly in a couple of layers of cling film, then put this into a resealable plastic bag and roll up tightly to exclude any air. Sugar Dough can be frozen in this way or stored in an airtight container at room temperature. This way, the paste will keep and be ready for use whenever you need it. (If you have frozen the paste, it must be thoroughly defrosted before use.) If the Sugar Dough feels a little stiff when you take it out, rub a little white vegetable fat over your hands and knead it well before use.

# Colouring Sugar Dough

Although Sugar Dough is available in a range of eleven colours, you can add food colour to it to create a whole spectrum. Food colours are available in three forms, paste, liquid and dust (powder) which can be used to create different effects. I have explained the uses of these colours below, which should help when you decide which is best for a particular purpose.

## Paste Colours

When deep or bright colours are required, I always use paste food colours because they are more concentrated and less likely to change the texture of the Sugar Dough than liquid food colourings. Add the paste colour a little at a time to the Sugar Dough using a cocktail stick, then knead well until the colour is even.

Remember that you can always make paste darker by adding more colour, but it is much more difficult to make it lighter. (However, a lighter shade can be achieved by adding White Sugar Dough to the coloured paste.)

You will find that the paste can stain your hands, so you may wish to wear a pair of food grade plastic gloves when colouring the paste.

Paste colours are also a good medium for painting onto Sugar Dough. Simply dilute the paste colour with cooled boiled water and paint onto the sugar. For a translucent effect, more water can be added, but do not add too much moisture to the surface of the Sugar Dough otherwise it will start to dissolve.

## Dust Colours

I love working with dust colours as they are easy to work with and lend themselves brilliantly to shading and adding highlights to Sugar Dough.

They are also ideal for painting sugar, particularly when you want it to dry quickly. Add clear alcohol (for example gin or vodka) to the dust for a smooth consistency. When you are working on a particular project, it is advisable to have a small paint palette to mix the colours. Although the liquid will evaporate fairly rapidly, there is no need to wash the leftover dust colour away before finishing the project as the addition of more alcohol will bring it back to painting consistency again the next time you need it.

The range of dust colours is incredible, so do try them as they will increase your artistic repertoire when working with sugar. Your work can be as pastel pretty or as dramatic as you like.

## Liquid Colours

If you are surface-painting Sugar Dough, liquid colours can be used instead of diluted paste colours. For example, where a pattern is required on an item of clothing, the liquid colour can simply be painted onto the sugar.

# Measuring Colours

If you are making a particular shade of paste, you may wish to record how much colour you have used so that the same colour can be made again. Always weigh the paste in the first instance, then measure the colour you are adding. If you are using liquid food colour, simply record the number of drops used. Recording the amount of paste or dust colour used is more difficult, so always keep a small swatch of the coloured paste for comparison. A set of measuring spoons is available which record a 'smidgen', a 'pinch' or a 'dash' (Lakeland Plastics), but if you can't get hold of these, try putting a certain amount on the end of a cocktail stick or spoon and record how many times colour must be added to obtain the required shade. As long as you weigh the Sugar Dough in the first instance, you can work from there. Always write down your colouring methods so that you can refer to them later.

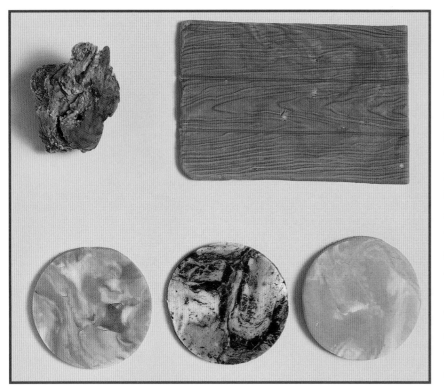

# Marbelling

Coloured Sugar Dough can be marbelled together to create a range of effects: I use marbelling for floors, marble pedestals, water, rocks and wood, for example. To marble two or more colours, roll a long sausage of each colour, then twist them together and roll into one big sausage. Roll this up, then form into a ball. Repeat the process until the desired effect is achieved, taking care not to blend the colours too much.

# Techniques

All of the projects in this book will require a cake and cake drum (board) to be covered (iced). If you are new to cake decorating, it is worth mastering these basic techniques as you will use them every time you decorate a cake.

## Covering a Cake Board

There are two ways in which a cake board can be covered, so choose whichever you prefer.

### Method 1

- Begin with a clean work surface - a large, non-stick polyethylene board is ideal. Rub a little white vegetable fat over the surface or dust with icing sugar (in a shaker).

- Knead the Sugar Dough with a little white vegetable fat on your hands until it is smooth and pliable. Form it into a smooth oval ball, then roll it out using a large polyethylene rolling pin, keeping in mind the shape you are trying to achieve.

- Hold the cake drum over the paste to see if it is large enough, if not continue to roll out.

- Brush the surface of the cake drum with a little cooled, boiled water. This will help the paste to stick, so it is important that the entire surface is moist.

- Lift the edge of the Sugar Dough over the rolling pin, pick up and lay over the cake drum.

- Smooth over the surface with a cake smoother, then trim off any excess with a small sharp knife, using a downward motion as you cut.

- Once you have completed the project, add a finishing touch to the cake drum by attaching a length of 15mm wide ribbon around the edge. Overlap the ends of the ribbon by 2cm or 3cm (about 1"), then secure in place with non-toxic stick glue or a little double-sided sticky tape.

### Method 2

- Knead and roll out the Sugar Dough as in Method 1.

- Brush around the outside of the cake drum with cooled, boiled water, leaving an area in the centre about the size of the cake. Lift the paste and lay over the drum.

- Smooth over the surface using a cake smoother. Using the tin in which the cake was baked as a template (or make a template from greaseproof paper), mark out the area where the cake will be. Remove the tin, then carefully cut out this centre section, ensuring it is slightly smaller than the covered cake. (It is better to make the cut out section too small rather than too big, otherwise you will be left with a gap around the cake.)

- Remove the paste from the centre of the board. This should not be stuck down as the centre of the board was not moistened.

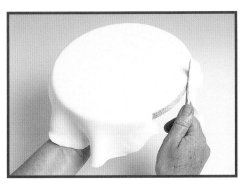

- Cut the excess paste from around the outside of the board and trim with ribbon once completed, as in Method 1.

# Covering a Cake

There are two main methods of covering a cake, one with a layer of marzipan and one without. If you are covering a rich fruit cake, it is important to follow the method using marzipan. If you are covering a Madeira cake or similar, either method can be used. Remember that the surface of the covered cake should be smooth and level for decorating.

## Method 1 (suitable for all cakes)

- Whether you are covering a sponge or fruit cake, the surface should be smooth and level. If there are any holes in the cake, fill them in with pieces of marzipan and flatten. Using a pastry brush, cover the surface of the cake with a thin layer of apricot glaze.

- Dust a clean surface with icing sugar, or you can use a thin film of vegetable fat. Never use cornflour, as this may become trapped and cause a mould to form. Roll out a piece of marzipan large enough to cover the top and sides of the cake and place over the cake. Trim off any excess with a sharp knife and smooth the surface with a cake smoother. Allow to dry for several hours, preferably overnight.

- Roll out the Sugar Dough as described for covering the board, making sure the piece is at least the diameter and twice the depth of the cake.

- Brush the marzipanned cake with clear alcohol, then lift the Sugar Dough over the cake without allowing it to stretch at the sides. Gently rub over the top with a cake smoother using a circular motion - this will adhere the Sugar Dough to the marzipan and give a good finish.

- The sides of the cake are always the most difficult to cover, especially if the cake is petal shaped or hexagonal. The main thing to avoid is tearing the Sugar Dough, so after you have laid the paste on the top of the cake, gently ease it against the sides of the cake using the side of your hand. If the cake is square, work on the corners first, then work on the sides of the cake. Always use the side/palm of your hand rather than your fingers as this area of your hand is much flatter and will create a smoother finish.

- Once the paste has adhered to the sides, take a cake smoother and place it against the side of the cake with the flat edge downwards, then hold against the side of the cake, working it backwards and forwards, pressing down on the work surface. This will thin out the excess Sugar Dough at the base of the cake. Trim off with a clean sharp knife. Run the cake smoother all around the sides to neaten. (If the cake is petal shaped or similar, you will not be able to use a cake smoother on the sides, so use the palm of your hand to create a good finish.)

- Finally, you can 'polish' the surface of the paste with the palm of your hand to give a nice shiny surface, if required.

- Place the cake on the board.

- Ideally the cake and board should be left to dry for at least 12 hours. The reason for this is that, if the paste is firm, it will be less likely to get marked or damaged while you are working, and any spillages can be wiped away without staining.

## Method 2 (suitable for sponge cakes, or similar)

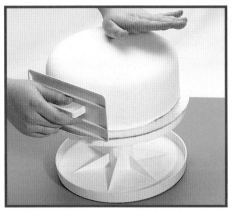

- Spread a thin layer of apricot glaze or buttercream over the entire surface of the cake.

- Roll out the Sugar Dough, as described above, and carefully lay it over the cake.

- Smooth the top of the cake and bring the paste down the sides, as before, then trim and use a smoother to create a good finish.

- Secure the cake to the board and leave to dry, as in Method 1.

# Essential Tools for Modelling

In addition to the basic tools required for covering a cake, you will find that there are many products on the market designed for sugar modelling: I have found that collecting tools and cutters becomes an obsession once you are bitten by the bug! However, there are certain tools which I never leave home without and I would recommend purchasing.

## Essential items:

Large and small polyethylene rolling pins

Cake smoother with handle

PME double-ended plain cutting wheel

Pizza cutter

Craft knife

Small sharp knife

Garlic crusher

Sugar shaper

Interchangeable design wheel

High quality paintbrushes

## PME modelling tools:

No. 1 - Bone Tool

No. 2 - Blade and Shell Tool

No. 3 - Ball Tool

No. 4 - Scallop and Comb Tool

No. 5 - Serrated and Tapered Cones Tool

No. 9 - Bulbous Cone Tool

No. 10 - Flower/Leaf Shaper Tool

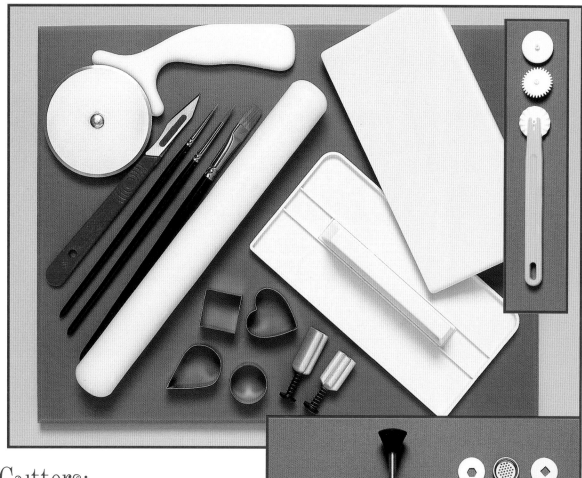

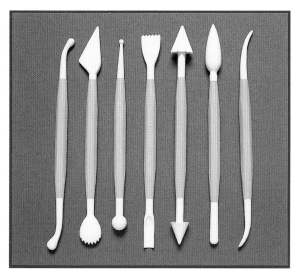

## Cutters:

Blossom plunger cutters (set of 3)

Heart shaped plunger cutters (set of 3)

Rose petal cutters (set of 4)

Briar rose circular cutters (set of 4)

Heart cutters (set of 3)

Plain round cutters (set of 8; 3cm-10cm)

## Edibles:

Selection of paste and dust food colourings

# Figure Modelling

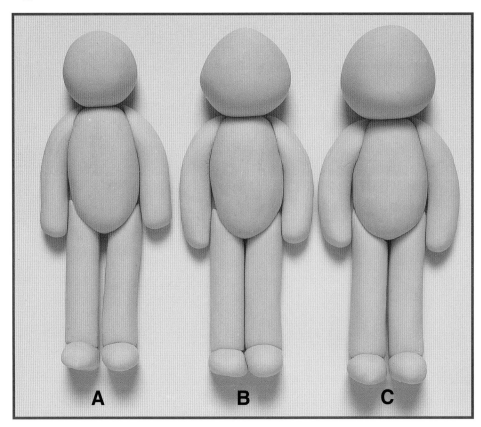

This section describes how to make the basic shapes required for figure modelling. By starting with the simplest of forms, you will have the foundations for making the types of figures described in the projects which follow. The component parts of a basic figure should be assembled in the following order: • body • legs • feet or shoes • clothing • arms and hands • collar • head • facial features • hair • accessories

However, for ease of reference, I have described how to model a basic figure starting at the head and working down, finishing with the feet.

## Basic Shapes for Modelling

The first basic shape to make for modelling is a spherical shape. By creating a ball with a smooth, crack-free surface, you can model cone, sausage and cigar shapes. From these basic shapes, you can make heads, body parts and animal shapes.

When using Sugar Dough, always make sure it is smooth and supple before you begin to model shapes or roll out. This can be achieved by kneading the paste for a few minutes.

## Making Heads

A head is simple to make: simply roll a smooth ball of paste. The difficult part, however, is getting the head in the correct proportion to the rest of the body. In reality, an adult human body is usually six or seven times the size of the head; for children, the head is slightly bigger in proportion to the body. When making figures, I tend to find that making the head a quarter or a fifth the size of the body (i.e. bigger than in reality) suits this style of figure modelling. Do always bear in mind that the proportions can be changed according to the subject.

These three models give a starting point of approximately how big the head should be in proportion to the body:

**A is too small**

**B is just right**

**C is too large**

# Making a Basic Face

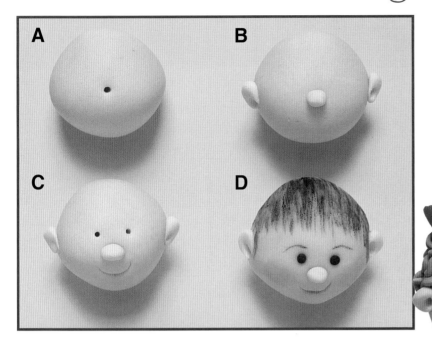

- Roll a smooth ball of Sugar Dough and make a small hole in the centre of the face for the nose (A).

- Roll two small teardrop shapes for the ears and attach to the sides of the head in line with the nose. Use the end of a paintbrush to secure and indent the ears. Make a small cone shape for the nose and glue into the hole (B).

- Mark two holes for the eyes with the end of a piece of raw spaghetti. The eyes should be just above and either side of the nose in a triangle shape. Fill the eye holes with small balls of Sugar Dough. Make a smile with a scalloped modelling tool, or if you require a bigger smile, indent with the edge of a small circle cutter (C).

- Outline the eyebrows with diluted paste food colour. Paint the mouth with pink or red paste food colour, then water some down further to blush the cheeks. If you prefer you can use pink lustre dust applied with a dry brush. Finally, paint on the hair using diluted paste food colour or extrude paste through a sugar shaper and secure with edible glue (D).

Putting things in the right and wrong place makes such a difference to final look of the face. These faces have the same components but look very different.

Face E: this face has oversized eyes, the features are too spaced out, the cheeks are too colourful and the ears are too high.

Face F: here, the eyes are too small and close together, the mouth is too far away from the nose and the ears are much too small.

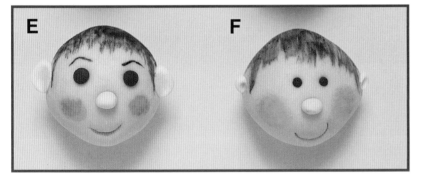

# Creating Facial Expressions

The faces below and overleaf show how a change of moustache, hairstyle, or smile can completely transform the look. You can give your models teeth, freckles, dimples, or a frown to add to their character. As your skills improve, you will have great fun creating your very own unique Sugar Dough characters.

# Facial Expressions

# Body Shapes

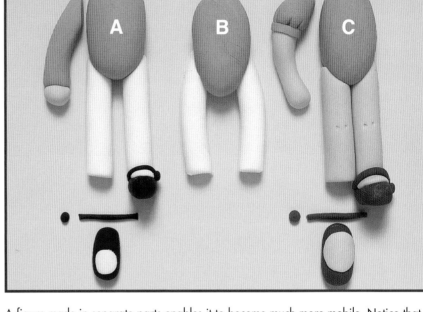

This shows the basic body shape for a baby or young child where the body and legs are made in one piece. A piece of raw spaghetti pushed into the body while the paste is still soft will support the head. This is the simplest way to model a figure. (The basic shape is the same for both male and female.)

A figure made in separate parts enables it to become much more mobile. Notice that the legs have a diagonal cut at the top, which gives a smooth fit at the hip line and keeps the legs in line with the body. Make sure the legs are not too high up as this will create a large gap in-between them (A).

This example makes a good base for a Victorian figure, young or old, wearing a longer dress where just the feet are showing (B). Here, it is not so important to ensure the legs are spaced correctly.

A 1940s style character with a short skirt or trousers looks cute with dimples in the legs, particularly for children (C).

# Arms and Hands

When making arms for a figure, they should start right at the top of the shoulder and come to about halfway down the thigh. Always ensure the arms are in the correct proportion before finishing off the detail. The easiest way to ensure they are the same length is to roll out one sausage of paste, measure it and make a cut in the centre (see Hints and Tips, page 20).

If the figure is wearing long sleeves, the hand and arm can be made separately, as follows:-

- Roll a long sausage of paste in the colour of the sleeves, then make a diagonal cut in the centre with a craft knife.

- Make two small balls of flesh coloured paste for the hands and secure to the end of

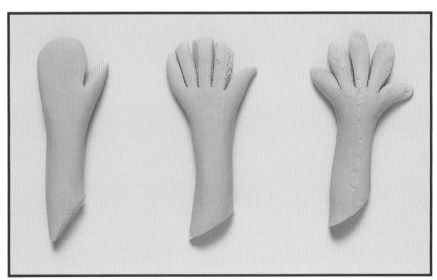

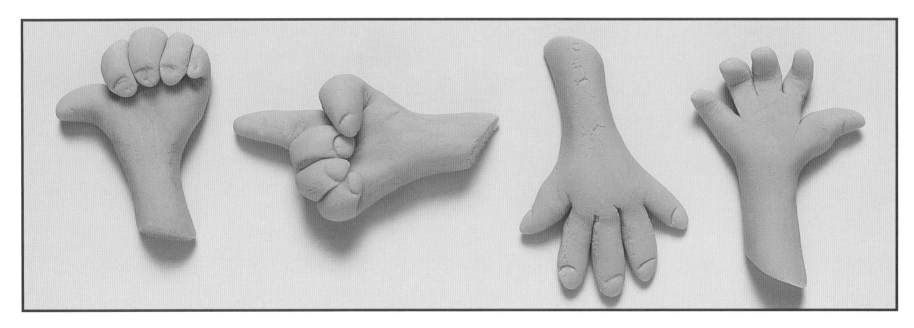

each arm. You may wish to insert a short piece of raw spaghetti into each wrist to support the hands further.

• Cut the fingers and thumb on each hand with a sharp knife, then carefully round off each digit and lengthen slightly using your fingers. Indent the palm of the hand to give it some shape.

If the figure has bare arms, you will need to model the arms and hands together, which takes a little more practice.

• Roll a piece of Sugar Dough into a ball, then roll out an even sausage shape to the thickness required. Make a cut in the centre, then check the length of the arms. If they are too long, cut paste from the straight edge, not the rounded end.

• Thin both arms at the wrist by rolling back and forth on the work surface with your finger. If the arms are bent, pinch the paste at the back of the elbow and carefully bend as required.

• Slightly flatten the hand and finish in the same way as before.

## Legs and Feet

When you are making the legs, always remember that they should start at the hip, rather than at the top of the thigh. In terms of proportion, the legs should be about the same length as the body and should be slightly thicker for male figures than for female.

• Roll out a long sausage of paste and cut in the centre. Make a steep diagonal cut at the top of each leg so that it fits at the hip.

• Flatten a section at the bottom of each leg for the foot. Thin the lower half of the leg, then shape the knee and ankle by rolling with your little finger.

• Shape the foot and mark the toes with the back of a knife. (There is no need to make feet if the figure is wearing shoes.)

If the figure is wearing trousers, simply make the legs in the same colour as the trouser material, as described opposite.

# Dressing Figures

If you have basic dressmaking skills, you will find them very helpful when cutting out and fitting sleeves and clothing in Sugar Dough. However, if you are completely new to the art, there are plenty of helpful tips which, combined with the basic skills, should make dressing figures in Sugar Dough achievable even for the complete beginner. Always bear in mind that you can make your characters' clothing as simple or as extravagant as you wish.

# Shirts and Bodices

It is always much easier to make the body the same colour you require for the bodice of the dress or shirt, thus eliminating the need for a top layer of clothing.

## Skirts

When making a skirt or petticoat, be it long or short, use the same basic method:

- Roll the required amount of Sugar Dough into a smooth ball, then into a thick sausage shape.

- Roll out to about 2mm (approximately $^1/_{16}$") thickness, then cut a curve at the top and bottom using a cutting wheel. (Curves usually fit much better than straight lines.)

- Gather the skirt along the top edge, keeping the curved shape. If you are finding it difficult to make folds, use the end of a paintbrush to gently lift and shape the paste.

- Finally, press the top edge down with your finger to fix the folds, then run the cutting wheel across the top once more to neaten the edge. Attach around the waist with edible glue.

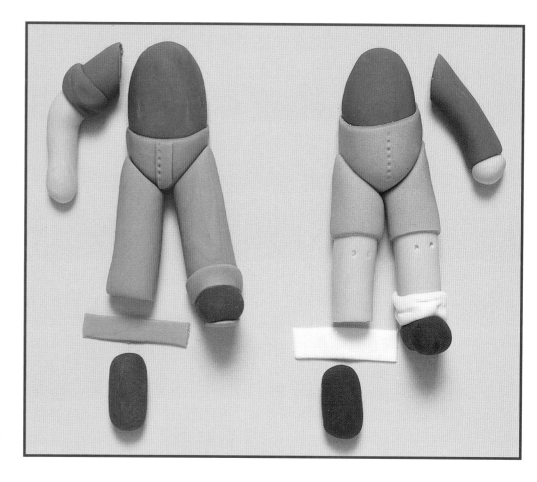

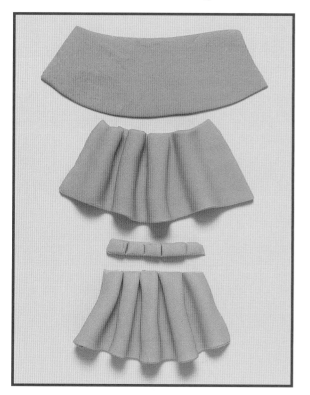

## Sleeves

Arms can be made of a solid colour to represent a long sleeve (as previously described), which eliminates the need to cover the arm. A short sleeve will require the arm and hand to be modelled in one piece and a short sleeve added to the top.

## Trousers

Cover the bottom half of the body to the waist in the trouser colour. For a long trouser, simply make the legs in the same colour as the trousers; there is no need to make flesh coloured legs underneath.

If you wish to make fitted trousers, make the legs and attach to the body then make the trousers as follows:

- Measure the distance from the waist to the ankle and from the inside leg to the outside where the seams will meet.

- Draw and cut out templates based on your measurements and cut out two pieces from Sugar Dough, one for the back and one for the front.

- Make a cut in the centre of each piece from the ankle to the top inside leg, then lay the paste over the body and tuck the paste around the legs. Secure along the seams.

- If you wish to have only one seam running along the inside of the leg, make the trousers in two parts, a left and a right, and wrap around the body and legs.

19

## Shorts

Colour the lower half of the body the colour required for the shorts. You can either make the legs in flesh coloured paste and wrap a piece of paste around the top of each leg in the colour of the shorts, or cut as desribed above for the trousers but with a short leg.

## Shoes

In most cases, there is no need to make elaborate shoes - a simple oval shape will do the job perfectly. Add simple decoration such as a strap and mark the heel on the sole of the shoe with the back of a knife. Remember to increase the proportions of the feet or shoes when making the legs thicker.

# Hints and Tips

 Although Sugar Dough is essentially a modelling medium, I have used it throughout the book to cover the cakes. You can, however, use sugarpaste (a ready-to-roll cake covering) to cover the cakes if you prefer.

 I always use edible glue to secure the modelled parts. Apply with a fine brush taking care not to put too much on to your work, as this will cause the pieces to slip. Tricky pieces can be supported with foam until dry.

 Most of the figures require a flesh coloured paste. The easiest way to make this is to add a little Peach Sugar Dough to White Sugar Dough.

 Where wires are used on cakes, they should never be pushed straight into the cake as they may cause injury if eaten accidentally. Where wires are required, push a posy pic (see stockists) into the cake and fill with the same colour paste as the surrounding area to cover the top. The wire can then be pushed into this paste. Alternatively, the wire can be pushed into the decoration which should be removed before the cake is eaten. It is important to ensure that the wire does not penetrate the cake. If the cake is to be given as a gift, it is important to inform the recipient if there are wires in the cake before it is eaten.

 Where pieces need extra support, raw spaghetti can be inserted into the Sugar Dough to keep the pieces together. As this is edible, it is perfectly safe to use but should be removed before the decorations are eaten.

 Although both icing sugar and white vegetable fat can be used to stop Sugar Dough from sticking to the work surface, I always use white vegetable fat because icing sugar can leave white marks on the paste.

 When you are using cutters, a little white fat smeared on the inside edge of the cutter will help the paste to slide off smoothly.

 When you are making arms and legs for a figure, roll out one long sausage shape in the required colour. Measure the length of the paste, then make a diagonal cut in the centre. As well as ensuring that both pieces are the same size, you can attach the diagonal end to the shoulders or hips.

 When you are making sugar flowers (as in "Away with the Fairies", for example), a useful yet simple skill to learn is how to make a 'Mexican hat'. Take a small ball of paste and mould it into a golf tee shape. Place the thick end onto a greased non-stick board and roll out the paste thinly with a paintbrush (or similar) so that you are left with a bump in the centre surrounded by a circular area of paste (hence the term 'Mexican hat'). Cut out the petals either freehand or using a cutter, ensuring that the bump stays in the middle as this will form the base of the flower. Thin the petals as required and remove from the board.

 When you are making a free-standing model, place it on a small moveable surface, such as a small non-stick board, when you are making it. This will allow you to move the piece around without handling it.

# Conversion Tables

These tables give conversions from metric to imperial. Although most products are sold in metric, some items are still generally referred to in imperial terms (for example, cake board sizes are usually given in inches). For quick conversions, the tables below give approximate values: measurements are rounded to the nearest 0.5cm and $\frac{1}{8}$" and weights to the nearest 5g and $\frac{1}{4}$oz.

| cm | inches | cm | inches |
|---|---|---|---|
| 0.5 | $\frac{1}{8}$ | 10 | 4 |
| 1 | $\frac{3}{8}$ | 12.5 | 5 |
| 1.5 | $\frac{5}{8}$ | 15 | 6 |
| 2 | $\frac{3}{4}$ | 18 | 7 |
| 2.5 | 1 | 20.5 | 8 |
| 3 | $1\frac{1}{8}$ | 23 | 9 |
| 4 | $1\frac{1}{2}$ | 25.5 | 10 |
| 5 | 2 | 28 | 11 |
| 6 | $2\frac{3}{8}$ | 30.5 | 12 |
| 7 | $2\frac{3}{4}$ | 33 | 13 |
| 8 | 3 | 35.5 | 14 |

| g | oz |
|---|---|
| 8 | $\frac{1}{4}$ |
| 15 | $\frac{1}{2}$ |
| 20 | $\frac{3}{4}$ |
| 30 | 1 |
| 45 | $1\frac{1}{2}$ |
| 60 | 2 |
| 100 | $3\frac{1}{2}$ |
| 200 | 7 |
| 455 | 1lb |
| 1kg | 2lb 3oz |

## Abbreviations

The abbreviations used in the book refer to the following manufacturers, full details of which can be found in the list of stockists on page 112:

**OP** = Orchard Products

**PME** = Precision Machining Engineers

**SK** = Squires Kitchen

## Materials

20cm (8") petal shaped cake

SK Sugar Dough in following amounts:

8g ($^1/_4$oz) Black

75g ($2^1/_2$oz) Green

80g ($2^3/_4$oz) Orange

20g ($^3/_4$oz) Red

570g (1lb 4oz) White

1.075kg (2lb 6oz) Yellow

SK Paste Food Colours: Berberis, Bulrush, Chestnut, Edelweiss, Poinsettia, Teddy Bear Brown

SK Edible Glue

SK Confectioners' Glaze

Raw spaghetti

## Equipment

33cm (13") hexagon cake drum

Non-stick board

Large rolling pin

Sharp knife

Small round cutter

Small heart cutter

PME small star plunger cutter

Florist wire: no. 22

Cutting wheel

PME modelling tools: scallop and comb tool, serrated and tapered cone tool

Paintbrush

2 posy pics

Red ribbon and red braid to trim

**IMPORTANT Some of the decorations on this cake contain wires. Ensure these are all removed before the cake is eaten.**

Everyone loves a teddy bear, so this cake would fit the bill for an office party or a birthday for any age.

## Covering the Cake and Board

1.  For the board, you will need 75g each of White, Green, Orange, and Yellow Sugar Dough. Make up 75g of pink by mixing a little SK Poinsettia Paste Food Colour into White Sugar Dough.

2.  Moisten the board with a little cooled, boiled water. Break each colour up into random small balls and push together on top of the board around the outside. Using a large rolling pin, roll out a section at a time directly on top of the board, forming a wide band all around the edge. Add more colours as you go along, leaving a circle in the centre slightly smaller than the cake. When the board is covered, trim off any excess paste.

3.  Cover the cake using 1kg of Yellow Sugar Dough, then secure the cake to the board with SK Edible Glue.

## Balloons

You will need to make four balloons in advance to allow them to dry before positioning on the cake. Cut out thick shapes of Sugar Dough oddments with small round and heart shaped cutters. Round off the edges. Push a length of no. 22 wire through the balloon, then add a tiny strip of paste at the base of each to prevent the balloon from slipping down the wire. Leave to dry flat.

## Sitting Teddy Bears

1.  To make the bears, colour 285g of White Sugar Dough with a little SK Bulrush and Chestnut Paste Food Colours until you have the desired shade.

2.  For each body, roll 20g into a cone shape, push a small piece of dry spaghetti into the neck, leaving

some showing to support the head. Using a PME comb tool, make stitch marks from the base to the middle, adding a belly button using a piece of raw spaghetti.

3. Make the legs from 10g of the brown paste rolled into a sausage shape. Push up at each end to flatten, then make a diagonal cut in the middle to create the top of each leg. Secure to each side of the body using SK Edible Glue.

4. For the arms, roll 10g into a sausage shape thinner than before, make a diagonal cut in the centre, and glue to either side of the dry spaghetti at the neck.

5. Make the head from 25g of the brown paste rolled into a smooth ball. Slide the head over the dry spaghetti and secure to the body with a dab of SK Edible Glue. Colour 30g of White Sugar Dough with SK Berberis Paste Food Colour for the snout and pads. Take off a small amount for each snout, roll into a cigar shape, flatten slightly and glue to the front of the teddy's face.

6. Press a PME comb tool gently into the paste to make stitch marks down the middle. Using the scalloped end of the same tool, mark either side of the line to create the mouth. Push a piece of dry spaghetti into the middle and pull down to create a smile.

7. Add two small balls of paste for the ears and flatten between your finger and thumb as you press onto the head.

8. Mark the eyes just above the snout and the nose at the top of the snout with a piece of dry spaghetti. Fill the eyes with small rounds of Black Sugar Dough. Make a nose with a cone shape of Black Sugar Dough and glue it into the hole.

9. Make four sitting teddies in total, arranging them in different positions just in front of the centre of the cake.

# Standing Teddy

1. Make the legs in the same way as before and lay them down on the work surface. Make the body as before and glue the legs on either side. Push a small piece of dry spaghetti into each foot and at the top of the body, leaving some showing, then set aside until dry. Glue the legs and body in an upright position to the the cake, pushing the dry spaghetti into the top of the cake to give support.

2. Make two arms and position the right one raised, supported with foam until dry, and secure the other around the back of the body.

3. Make the head and finish in the same way as before. Add a bow tie using any oddment of colour.

4. Push a posy pic between the back of the standing teddy and his left arm as soon as possible before it dries out then add three balloons. The other balloon can also be positioned on one of the sitting teddies at this stage, again using a posy pic.

24

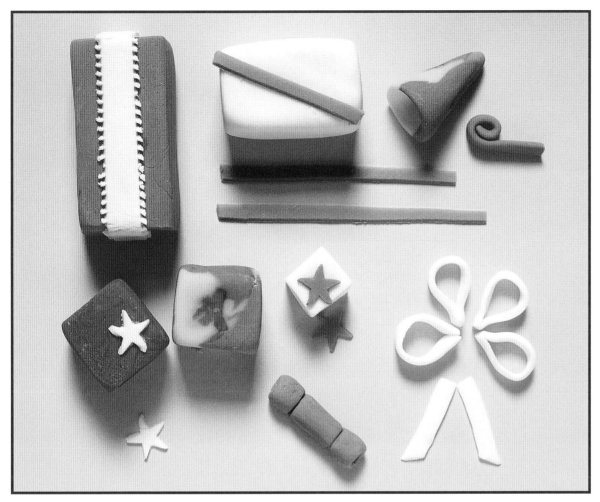

# Crackers

Using a small amount of Green and Orange Sugar Dough, roll a sausage shape 3cm long. Hollow out at each end with the end of a paintbrush and mark with the back of a knife. Secure in place.

# Presents

1. For the back of the cake, make one pink present using 35g of Sugar Dough and decorate with White Sugar Dough 'ribbon'. Make a second present using White Sugar Dough and decorate with green stripes and ribbons. Make a third smaller present using 15g of Red Sugar Dough decorated with white stars and ribbon. Secure in place with SK Edible Glue.

2. Make two further presents for the front of the cake using 15g for each and one tiny one using 4g of White Sugar Dough, decorated with orange stars and ribbons, as shown.

# Finishing Touches

Brush SK Confectioners' Glaze onto the balloons and any other decorations where you would like to add a shine.

# Party Hats

 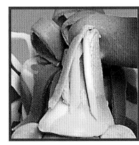 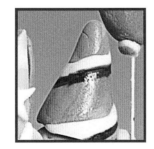 

Using leftover paste from the board, roll a small ball and push it over the smooth end of a PME tapered cone modelling tool, creating a hollow cone shape. Widen the edges to fit the teddy's head and attach in place with SK Edible Glue. Make four hats in total and decorate as desired.

# Party Hooters

Using the same Sugar Dough as the hats, make a thin sausage shape, flatten and curl up at one end. Push a small piece of dry spaghetti carefully into the end and leave to dry. When dry, push the spaghetti into the teddy's mouth.

# A Day in the Country

This contented shepherd is enjoying a peaceful moment in the field with all his companions! For me, this scene evokes many happy childhood memories of holidays on a farm.

## Materials

25.5cm (10") round cake

SK Sugar Dough in following amounts:

220g (7³/₄oz) Black

50g (1³/₄oz) Blue

15g (¹/₂oz) Brown

1.25kg (2lb 12oz) Green

8g (¹/₄oz) Peach

1.02kg (2lb 4oz) White

SK Paste Food Colours: Berberis, Blackberry, Bulrush, Holly Ivy, Marigold, Poinsettia, Teddy Bear Brown

SK Edible Glue

Raw spaghetti

## Equipment

33cm (13") round cake drum

Non-stick board

Large and small rolling pins

Basket weave textured rolling pin

Sharp knife

PME modelling tools: scallop and comb tool, flower and leaf shaper tool

Design wheel

2cm (³/₄") round cutter

5cm (2") round fluted cutter

4cm (1¹/₂") leaf cutter

Paintbrushes (various)

Cocktail stick

Dark green ribbon to trim

## Covering the Cake and Board

1. Knead 1.25kg of Green Sugar Dough. Cut off 500g and cover the board.

2. Roll out the remaining Green Sugar Dough and cover the cake. Set aside any excess paste to be used for decorations later. Secure the cake to the board: it will need to be off-centre to allow room at the front for the lambs.

3. Take 50g of Blue Sugar Dough and mix with 200g of White Sugar Dough to create a marbled effect. Roll out and cut out four shapes for the sky using the template (page 109). Soften all the edges with your finger and secure around the side of cake using SK Edible Glue. Overlap each section until the cake is covered. Keep any leftover pieces and put aside.

## Lambs

1. For the lambs you will need 500g of White Sugar Dough. To make a body roll 40g into a ball then form a smooth oval shape. Using a sharp knife, make a split at each end, as shown overleaf. Gently pull out each section for the legs and round off the edges with your fingers. (Note that one sheep at the back of the cake only has half a body.)

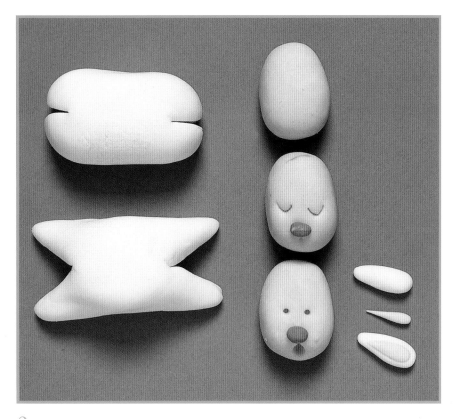

4. Make a small sausage shape from White Sugar Dough for each tail, mark with a comb modelling tool and glue to the body.

5. Colour 60g of White Sugar Dough a flesh colour by mixing with a little Peach Sugar Dough. Make two heads and mark the faces as shown. Make another head in the same way using Black Sugar Dough.

6. For the ears, make two teardrop shapes from a small amount of White Sugar Dough, make a very thin flesh coloured teardrop shape for the inside and press together. Cut a 2cm circle, glue to the back of the head and mark with a comb modelling tool. Add curls made from tiny, twisted sausage shapes of White Sugar Dough. Secure to the top of the head with SK Edible Glue. Colour a small amount of White Sugar Dough pink with a little SK Poinsettia Paste Food Colour and make a nose.

7. Secure all the lambs in place on the cake and board with SK Edible Glue.

2. Continue to model the legs according to the position you require for each sheep. Roughen the surface of the whole body using a PME comb modelling tool.

3. To make all the hooves you will need 20g of Black Sugar Dough. Take off a small amount for each, roll into a sausage shape and chop into four, then glue to each leg.

## Sheepdogs

1. You will need 100g of Black and 30g of White Sugar Dough to complete both dogs. To make the sitting dog, take 20g of Black Sugar Dough and roll into a cone shape for the body. Push a small piece of dry spaghetti into the top to support the head.

2. Divide 8g of Black Sugar Dough in half for the back legs and roll both pieces into a cone shape. Glue to the body using SK Edible Glue. Add two small balls of White Sugar Dough for the paws and mark with the back of a knife.

3. Make two front legs using 8g of White Sugar Dough. Roll the paste into a sausage shape 8cm long, push up at each end with your finger to make a paw, then make a diagonal cut in the centre to make two legs. Secure these to the front of the body with SK Edible Glue.

4. Roll out a small piece of White Sugar Dough and cut out the piece of fur to go onto the chest using a leaf cutter. Mark with a knife, then glue over the top of the legs.

5. For the head, roll 8g of Black Sugar Dough into a cone shape. Roll out some White Sugar Dough and cut out the front section of the face using the 4cm leaf cutter. Place over the centre of the head and shape around the nose and under the mouth area, as shown. Slide the head over the dry spaghetti.

6. Mark the centre front of the head with the back of a knife, then push the end of a paintbrush into the base of the line and pull down slightly to open the mouth. Add a tiny pink teardrop shape for the tongue and mark in the centre with a knife. Add a small black ball for the nose. Make holes for the eyes with a piece of dry spaghetti, then fill these with tiny round balls of White Sugar Dough coloured with SK Marigold Paste Food Colour. Using a fine paintbrush, paint on pupils with SK Blackberry Paste Food Colour.

7. Make two ears from 5g of Black Sugar Dough divided equally. Roll two small sausage shapes and secure to the head with SK Edible Glue. Curl the ears forwards.

8. For the tail, roll a small sausage of Black Sugar Dough and make a white tip for the end. Roll the colours together and secure to the dog so that the tail is pointing upwards. Secure the completed dog to the left side of cake with SK Edible Glue.

9. Make the lying dog using the same method and secure in place.

# Puppy

Make a small puppy using the same method as for the dogs but reducing the amount of paste used.

# Bale of Hay

Take 85g of White Sugar Dough and colour with a mixture of SK Berberis and Marigold Paste Food Colours to make a straw colour. Take off 65g and set the rest aside. Shape the paste into an oblong shape and mark with a knife to resemble straw. Using a cocktail stick, prick each end of the bale to roughen the surface. Secure to the right side of the cake.

# Shepherd's Body and Legs

1. Colour 100g of White Sugar Dough with a touch of SK Teddy Bear Brown Paste Food Colour to make an off-white shade. Take off 25g for the body and set the remainder to one side.

2. Roll an oval shape for the body then push a stick of dry spaghetti into the centre, leaving a little showing at the top to support the head. Make the trousers from 25g of White Sugar Dough tinted with Teddy Bear Brown Paste Food Colour. Roll into a sausage shape 11cm long. Cut diagonally in the centre and make a straight edge at each end. Secure to the body with SK Edible Glue.

3. Divide 10g of Brown Sugar Dough in half to make the shoes. Roll two ovals and glue to the bottom of the legs.

4. Make the crook from a tiny piece of Brown Sugar Dough. Roll into a long thin sausage shape and form a crook at the top. Glue to the cake in front of the shepherd.

5. Using a fine paintbrush and SK Bulrush Paste Food Colour, paint a check design on the trousers.

# Shepherd's Smock

1. To make the shepherd's smock, roll out some of the remaining off-white coloured Sugar Dough and cut out a rectangle measuring 5cm x 15cm. Run a design wheel along the lower edge to create stitch marks. Make three gathers in the centre of this piece,

29

then fit around the body at chest height, wrapping over at the back neatly. Cut out a 2cm x 1.5cm rectangle for the top section of the smock and make stitch marks with the design wheel. Cut out two 2.5cm x 2cm rectangles for the collar and edge with stitch marks. Do not attach the collar until the arms are in place.

2. Using 10g of the off-white coloured paste, roll a sausage shape, then make a diagonal cut in the centre for the arms. Make a straight cut at each end for the wrist. Secure to the body with SK Edible Glue and bring forward. Secure the puppy in place over the shepherd's right arm.

# Shepherd's Head and Hands

1. For the head, take 15g of flesh coloured Sugar Dough and roll into a rounded teardrop shape. Slide the head over the dry spaghetti on top of the body. Add the facial features, using tiny balls of White Sugar Dough for the eyes, two small teardrop shapes of flesh coloured paste for the ears and a PME scallop tool to mark the smile. Paint the pupils with SK Black Paste Food Colour, then paint the eyebrows with SK Bulrush Paste Food Colour. Blush the cheeks with diluted SK Poinsettia Paste Food Colour.

2. For the hands, roll two small balls of flesh paste and flatten slightly. Using a sharp knife mark a thumb and four fingers. Pull out gently and round off the edges, glue the hand to the wrist and place on the puppy.

3. For the beard, add a small amount of White to some leftover SK Teddy Bear Brown Sugar Dough to lighten. Cut out a small half-moon shape using small circle cutters, then mark all the way around with a sharp knife and glue to the face. Fill a sugar shaper with the same colour and extrude some strands using the disc with the largest holes. Attach short lengths around the back and sides of the head.

4. For the hat, use 20g of Sugar Dough left over from the hay bale. Cut a 5cm circle and roll over with a basket weave rolling pin (if required). Cut a small circle in the centre to fit the head, then place a small cylinder of paste on the top for the crown of the hat.

# Bluebirds

1. Take 20g of the blue paste used for the sky and model the bluebirds, as shown. Begin by rolling the body into a cone shape, flatten the tail area with your fingers, then tilt the tail upwards. Make three tiny teardrop shapes and arrange on the tail. Make two flat cone shapes for the wings and mark with a knife for feathers.

2. Roll a small ball for the head and glue to the body. Mark the eyes with dry spaghetti, then secure little balls of White Sugar Dough inside. Make a tiny cone shape of SK Marigold coloured Sugar Dough for the beak, then split with a knife to open it up. Attach in place with SK Edible Glue, then position on the cake.

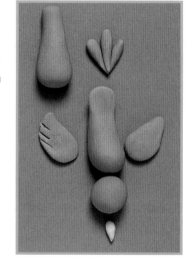

# Grass and Flowers

1. Take any leftover pieces of Green Sugar Dough and add a little SK Holly Ivy Paste Food Colour to create a deeper shade of green. Fill a sugar shaper with the paste and extrude short lengths for the tufts of grass and attach in place.

2. To make the flowers, roll out a scrap of SK Marigold coloured paste and cut out a number of shapes using blossom plunger cutters. Fill the centre of the flowers with a tiny round of pink coloured paste. Secure in place.

3. Using SK Holly Ivy Paste Food Colour and a stiff brush, stipple the cake here and there to add texture.

# Victorian Toy Box

## Materials

20cm (8") round cake

SK Sugar Dough in following amounts:

30g (1oz) Black

140g (5oz) Blue

55g (2oz) Brown

425g (15oz) Green

60g (2oz) Orange

4g (1/8oz) Peach

680g (1lb 8oz) Red

345g (12oz) White

200g (7oz) Yellow

SK Paste Food Colours: Berberis and Poinsettia

SK Baber Folk Paints: Blue, Brown, Black and Red

SK Edible Glue

SK Confectioners' Glaze

Raw spaghetti

## Equipment

33cm (13") round cake drum

Non-stick board

Large rolling pin

Taffeta veining rolling pin

Thin rolling pin (optional)

Sharp knife

PME modelling tools: blade and shell tool, scallop and comb tool

Cutting wheel

Sugar shaper

Small round cutter

2.3cm (7/8") square cutter

2cm (6/8") square cutter

Letter cutters (optional)

Fine and medium paintbrushes

Plastic ruler

Blue ribbon to trim

Recently I redecorated my own doll's house and bought a new toy box for the nursery. As I filled it up with toys, I thought it would make a splendid subject for a cake. The wonderful vibrant colours of Sugar Dough work perfectly here to reproduce the Victorian toys.

## Covering the Cake and Board

1. Roll out 400g of Green Sugar Dough and cover the board.

2. Take 600g of Red Sugar Dough and cover the cake.

3. Colour 110g of White Sugar Dough with SK Berberis Paste Food Colour to make a cream shade. Cut out a 20cm diameter circle of paste for the top of the cake. This can be measured using a cake board, or you can make your own template from greaseproof paper. Secure this on top of the cake using SK Edible Glue.

## Side Decoration

1. Knead 120g of Yellow Sugar Dough, roll out and cut two strips measuring 38cm x 2cm to go around the top and bottom of the cake. Secure in place with SK Edible Glue.

2. Roll out 50g of Blue Sugar Dough and cut out 50 squares using a 2cm square cutter. Place them in-between the yellow bands.

3. Mark the yellow band at the top of the cake at 9cm intervals, then mark the bottom yellow band at points in-between to indicate where to position the ropes.

4. For the ropes you will require 50g of White Sugar Dough. Soften the paste and extrude through a sugar shaper with a large hole disc. Each rope should measure 9cm when twisted. Glue the ends of each piece of rope to the markings at the top and bottom of the cake.

# Toy Box

1. Mix 80g of Blue Sugar Dough with 100g of White. Roll out to a thickness of 8mm using a taffeta veining rolling pin to give a wood effect. Cut out two rectangular pieces measuring 10cm x 4cm for the front and back, two pieces measuring 6cm x 4cm for the sides and one piece for the lid measuring 10cm x 6cm.

2. Bevel both ends of the back, front and sides so that they fit together neatly when dry. Press the edge of a ruler across all the pieces to mark two planks. Leave to dry.

3. Assemble the toy box and secure in place on top of the cake. Finally, glue the lid into an upright position and support with foam if necessary until dry.

# Soldier

1. To make the body, roll 30g of Red Sugar Dough into a cone shape 7cm long. Place this down on a non-stick board to dress.

2. Take 10g of Red Sugar Dough and roll into a long sausage shape for the arms. Make a diagonal cut in the centre, make another diagonal cut at the wrist, then glue to each side of the body.

3. Decorate the jacket using a tiny piece of Yellow Sugar Dough. Roll out a thin strip of paste and create a fringe with a sharp knife. Glue around each shoulder, then top with a small oval shape.

4. Add the braid and buttons to the front of the jacket and put a small strip around the wrist. When the body has hardened off, stand it inside the toy box, securing with SK Edible Glue. Push a piece of spaghetti into the top.

5. For the head, add a little Peach Sugar Dough to 15g of White Sugar Dough to make a flesh colour. Take a tiny piece of the paste and place to one side (this will be for the nose and ears), then roll the remainder into a smooth ball. Secure the head to the body.

6. Add two small teardrop shapes for the ears. Make a thin twist of yellow for the chin strap and glue around the face. Add the facial features, filling the eyes with tiny balls of Brown Sugar Dough. Paint the eyebrows using a fine brush and SK Brown Baber Folk Paint. Blush the cheeks with diluted SK Poinsettia Paste Food Colour.

7. Make the busby using 20g of Black Sugar Dough rolled into a smooth oval shape, then cut a straight edge at one end. Hollow out this end with your finger or a thin rolling pin, opening it out slightly to fit snugly over the head. Attach in place, then add a yellow button to each end of the chin strap to finish. When dry, brush with SK Confectioners' Glaze.

# Clown

1. Roll 25g of Yellow Sugar Dough into a cone shape measuring 6cm for the body. Using a tiny amount of Red Sugar Dough, make three buttons and glue them down the front. (The easiest way is to apply SK Edible Glue to the body using a fine paintbrush.) Leave the body to harden off, then glue into position in the toy box.

2. To make the arms, roll 15g of Yellow Sugar Dough into a sausage shape. Make a diagonal cut in the middle and glue to the top of the body, placing the right arm over the box.

3. Make a frill to fit around the wrist from a tiny piece of Yellow Sugar Dough

rolled into a narrow strip. Gather the paste along one side and glue to the wrist using SK Edible Glue.

4. Take 15g of White Sugar Dough and pinch off enough to make two small balls for the hands. Using the remainder, roll out a strip measuring 11cm x 2cm for the neck frill. Gather along one side and glue to the top of the body.

5. For the head, roll 20g of White Sugar Dough into a smooth ball and glue to the body. Add two small balls pinched between your finger and thumb for the ears. Make a hole for the nose in the centre of the face and fill with a ball of Red Sugar Dough. Mark the eyes above the nose, but make them wider apart than usual. Using

the back of a knife, make a cross over the top, then fill the eyes with tiny balls of Black Sugar Dough. Paint the cheeks with watered down SK Poinsettia Paste Food Colour and paint on a smile.

6. For the hair, soften 10g of Brown Sugar Dough with a little water and fill a sugar shaper. Extrude strands through a fine hole disc and cut into small tufts for the hair, then arrange over the ears and secure in place with SK Edible Glue.

7. Make a hat from a small circle and a small ball of Black Sugar Dough. Secure the circle in place, then place the ball on the top.

# Horse

1. Roll out 20g of White Sugar Dough to approximately 0.5cm thickness and cut out the horse using the template (page 109). Paint on the mane and facial features using a fine paintbrush and SK Black Baber Folk Paint. Paint the bridle with SK Red Baber Folk Paint.

2. For the stick, roll a thin strip of Red Sugar Dough around an 8cm length of dry spaghetti, then push the stick into the neck of the horse. Make the reins from a thin strip of Red Sugar Dough and glue to the head. Position the completed horse inside the box.

# Rag Doll

1. For the body, roll 15g of Orange Sugar Dough into a cone shape and glue to the top of the box.

2. Make two arms from 10g of White Sugar Dough equally divided, then roll each piece into a cone shape and glue the thickest end to the body, arranging the arms over the box. Make approximately 15g of flesh coloured Sugar Dough by mixing a little Peach into White, then set aside two thirds of the paste. Using one third of the paste, make two hands by rolling two small balls of paste, then flatten slightly and cut out a thumb shape on each with a sharp knife. Round off and indent the hand, then glue to the wrist.

3. Add a thin strip of Orange Sugar Dough around the wrist and secure in place. Paint a few blue spots onto the arms using a fine paintbrush and SK Blue Baber Folk Paint.

4. For the head, roll the remaining flesh coloured paste into a smooth ball. Mark out the face and complete in the same way as for the soldier. For the mouth, paint on a smile using diluted SK Poinsettia Paste Food Colour.

5. Soften 20g of Orange Sugar Dough and fill the sugar shaper. Extrude the strands as before and arrange around the head. Add two bunches to each side and secure in place. Make two tiny bows from Blue Sugar Dough and attach to the hair to hide the joins.

# Teddy Bear

1. To make the bear, you will need to mix together 20g each of Brown, Orange and Yellow Sugar Dough. This should give you a toffee colour. Take 15g of the paste and roll into an oval shape for the body. Glue into position on top of the cake at the front of the toy box.

2. For the legs, roll 15g into a sausage shape and turn up at each end for the feet. Cut in half and glue the legs to the base of the body.

3. For the arms, roll 10g of the brown paste into another sausage shape. Again, cut in half and secure to the top of the body. Arrange the limbs as required, using the main picture as a guide.

4. For the head roll 15g of brown paste into a ball and glue to the body. Make two small ears from a small ball flattened between your finger and thumb.

5. To make the lighter parts of the bear, colour a little White Sugar Dough with a hint of SK Berberis Paste Food Colour. Make the snout from a very small oval shape and secure in the centre of the head. Add stitch marks in the centre of the head with a PME comb modelling tool. Make a smile each side of the line using the scalloped end of the same tool. Make two holes for the eyes using a piece of spaghetti and fill with Brown Sugar Dough, then add a ball of Black Sugar Dough for the nose.

# Sitting Doll

1. Roll 10g of Green Sugar Dough into an oval shape for the body and secure to the front of the toy box.

2. Make two legs from small pieces of White Sugar Dough, each 4cm long. Make two small shoes from Brown Sugar Dough as shown and mark the heel with the back of a knife. Glue a foot to each leg and finish with a strap around the ankle, then attach the legs to the body.

3. For the skirt, roll out 10g of Green Sugar Dough into a strip measuring 10cm x 2.5cm. Gather at the top and fit around the waist, securing in place with SK Edible Glue.

4. For the apron, collar and hat, roll out a small piece of White Sugar Dough. Cut out strips of paste for the apron and fit them onto the front of the body. For the collar, cut out a small circle then cut this in half and place both pieces on top of the apron straps.

5. Colour 6g of White Sugar Dough with Peach to create a flesh colour. Roll into a ball for the head and mark the face as before. Roll out a small piece of White Sugar Dough and cut out a small circle for the hat. Glue the centre of the circle to the head with SK Edible Glue and lift the edges with the end of a paintbrush to create a loose frill.

# Train

You will need 25g each of Red and Blue Sugar Dough and 5g of Yellow Sugar Dough. Make blocks for the carriages, secure in place, then fill the back truck with multi-coloured pieces of Sugar Dough.

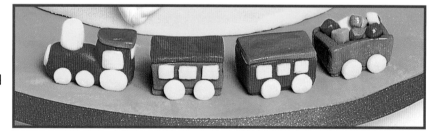

# Building Blocks

You will need 5g each of Red, Blue, Green and Yellow Sugar Dough. Cut out four squares in each colour using a 2cm square cutter. Glue them together to make a square. Add letters of your choice on the side to finish and attach to the top of the cake.

# Ball

Roll together small pieces of any leftover colour you have used into a ball. (I have used Yellow, Red and Orange Sugar Dough.) Attach to the top of the cake, next to the doll.

## Materials

25.5cm x 20cm (10" x 8") and 15cm x 10cm (6" x 4") oval cakes

SK Sugar Dough in following amounts:

15g (1/2oz) Black

100g (3 1/2oz) Orange

2.73kg (6lb) White

200g (7oz) Yellow

20g (3/4oz) SK White Sugar Florist Paste (SFP)

SK Paste Food Colours: Blackberry, Gentian, Leaf Green, Marigold, Poinsettia and Sunflower

SK Dust Food Colour: Violet

SK Metallic Lustre Dusts: Brilliant Gold, Burnt Copper

SK Edible Glue

SK Gildesol

SK Confectioners' Glaze

Raw spaghetti

## Equipment

35.5cm x 30.5 (14" x 12") oval cake drum

Non-stick board

Large and small rolling pins

Ribbed rolling pin

Taffeta veining rolling pin

Sharp knife

PME modelling tool: scallop and comb tool

Sugar shaper

Cutting wheel

Design wheel

3cm, 4cm and 10cm (1 1/2", 1 1/8" and 4") round cutters

5cm and 5.5cm (2" and 2 1/8") oval cutters

Rose petal cutter

Blossom plunger cutters

Medium and fine paintbrushes

Cocktail stick

Pink and pale blue ribbon to trim

# The Uninvited Guests

What appears to be a peaceful wedding is actually being disrupted by a few naughty ducks! If you are making this cake for a wedding, you can add as many tiers as is required for the number of guests.

## Covering the Cakes and Board

1. Colour 550g of White Sugar Dough with SK Leaf Green Paste Food Colour until you have a pale green colour. Cover the cake drum, then edge with pink ribbon. Allow to dry.

2. For the larger cake you will require 1kg of White Sugar Dough. Divide equally into three parts: leave one part white, colour the second part a deep shade of SK Gentian blue, and the third part a paler shade of SK Gentian. Marble these three colours together, take off a little piece of paste for the decorations and cover the cake in the usual way. Place the cake off-centre on the board, leaving a 5cm gap from the back edge of the board. Edge the base of the cake with a narrow ribbon.

3. For the smaller cake, colour 350g of White Sugar Dough with SK Marigold Paste Food Colour and cover the cake. Secure this cake off-centre on top of the larger one, leaving a 3cm gap from the back edge. Use the leftovers to make a number of small teardrops and attach with SK Edible Glue around the base.

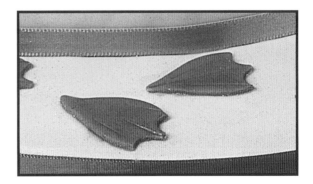

4. Roll out 30g of Orange Sugar Dough and cut out a number of footprints using the template (page 109) as a guide.

# Bridegroom Goose

1. To make the body, roll 100g of White Sugar Dough into a smooth ball, then into a cone shape. Model the thick end into a tail and cut out the tail feathers with the pointed end of a rose petal cutter, as shown. Position on top of the cake and insert a piece of dry spaghetti down the neck, leaving some showing to support the head.

2. Divide 15g of Orange Sugar Dough in half and make two legs. Secure to the sides of the body and place into position at the front of the cake.

3. For the wings, take 20g of White Sugar Dough and split in half. Roll each piece into a smooth, curved cone shape and mark with the back of a knife, as shown. Allow to firm,

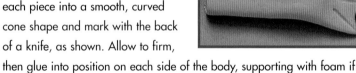

then glue into position on each side of the body, supporting with foam if necessary.

4. To make the head, roll 20g of White Sugar Dough into a teardrop shape. Place this over the dry spaghetti at the neck and secure with SK Edible Glue. Make the beak from a tiny piece of Orange Sugar Dough. Form a cone shape then flatten at the thick end with your finger. Push a small piece of dry

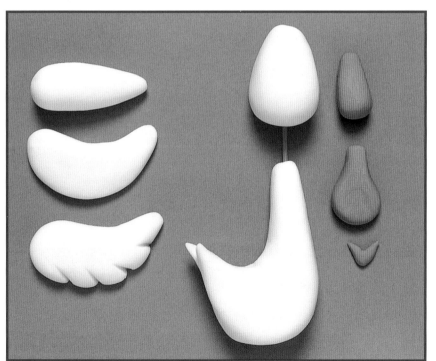

spaghetti into the end and push into the face. Make a small cigar shape for the lower beak, curve in the centre and glue under the beak.

5. Apply a coat of SK Confectioners' Glaze to the beak and legs to give extra shine.

## Waistcoat

Mix 30g of White Sugar Dough with a small amount of Black Sugar Dough to make a light grey colour. Cut off half the paste and set the rest aside. Roll out into a 6cm square and run a ribbed rolling pin over the paste to texture. Using the template (page 109), cut out the waistcoat shape. Cut two tiny oblong shapes for the pocket tops and glue diagonally at the front. Cut a narrow band measuring 4cm x 1cm to go around the back from one side of the waistcoat to the other. Glue into place on the body using SK Edible Glue.

## Collar and Tie

Cut out a strip of White Sugar Dough measuring 7cm x 1cm, glue around the neck above the waistcoat and turn down at the corners. Using a leftover piece of the blue paste, cut a strip measuring 2.5 x 1.5cm for the tie. Cut diagonally at the lower edge, pinch at the top to narrow and top with a small ball for the knot. Attach with SK Edible Glue then paint on stripes with a fine paintbrush using SK Gentian Paste Food Colour.

## Top Hat

Take the remaining grey paste and cut out the pieces for the top hat using the templates (page 109). Glue the pieces together, then make the hat band in a paler shade of grey by adding a little more White Sugar Dough. Check that it will fit the head, then set aside to dry.

# Goose Bride

1. Make the body, head, legs and wings in the same way as for the groom.

2. Make a small garter by frilling a narrow strip of White Sugar Dough with a cocktail stick. Make a thin roll of leftover blue paste in the centre and fit around the leg.

3. For the skirt, roll out 20g of White Sugar Dough into a strip measuring 9cm x 2cm. Run the wavy edge of a design wheel down one side, then make two rows of dots on the lower edge using the end of a piece of raw spaghetti. Frill the paste using a cocktail stick and arrange to fit all around the body. Finish with a narrow strip of blue around the waist.

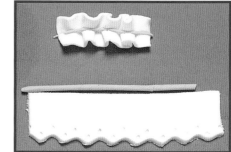

## Necklace

Roll several tiny round balls of White Sugar Dough and allow to dry. Dust with SK Burnt Copper Metallic Lustre Dust and glue around the bride's neck.

## Veil

Roll out 20g of White SFP very thinly, texture with a taffeta veining rolling pin, then cut out two 10cm circles. Fold one edge over to the other loosely to make a semi-circle. Gather the edge to fit the head and set aside. Take the other circle and cut out a semi-circle at one edge. Gather up the paste on this edge to fit the head. Glue firmly into position at the back and support with foam until dry. Add the short veil over the top and secure with SK Edible Glue. Add a tuft of hair by extruding a little softened White Sugar Dough through a fine hole disc in a sugar shaper.

# Bridesmaids

1. For each bridesmaid, make the body, head, legs and wings in exactly the same way as the bride but make them slightly smaller.

2. Colour 25g of White Sugar Dough with SK Poinsettia Paste Food Colour and make a skirt as before but with a straight edge. Gather and fit as described for the bride, then finish with a waistband and a bow at the back.

3. Make a dress for the other bridesmaid from White Sugar Dough, this time making two layers. Attach in place and dust with SK Violet Dust Food Colour.

4. Blush the cheeks of the geese with diluted SK Poinsettia and paint on the eyes with SK Blackberry Paste Food Colour.

# Pageboy

Again, make in the same way as the other geese, adding a top hat as for the groom.

# Bouquet and Flowers

1.  For the bridesmaids' flowers, make a 'Mexican hat' (see Hints and Tips, page 20) for the bouquet, turn over, place a small ball into the centre and fill with flowers made with a medium sized blossom plunger cutter. When you have cut out the flowers, roll a cocktail stick over the edges to thin and add a small ball for the centre.

2.  For the bride's flowers, make a Mexican hat, then cut out a leaf shape with a rose petal cutter, cover this with blossoms and secure with SK Edible Glue to the Mexican hat.

3.  Make more flowers in the same way and secure around the head of the bride and bridesmaids.

# Uninvited Guests

1. To make all the ducks, you will need 200g of Yellow Sugar Dough mixed with a little SK Sunflower Paste Food Colour. For each body, roll 25g into a cone shape, as shown. Press the back of a knife into the paste to mark the legs at the thickest end and mould each thigh with your fingers, gently pulling them out. Position each duck in the appropriate pose, then push a piece of dry spaghetti into the neck.

2. Make wings for each duck from 8g of Sugar Dough divided equally. Roll into a paddle shape and flatten at the end with your finger. Bend at the elbow and mark the feathers with a knife. Attach to the body with SK Edible Glue.

3. Roll each head from 15g of Sugar Dough. Gently push the head over the spaghetti and secure with SK Edible Glue. Roll two small balls for the cheeks and glue to the face.

4. Make the legs, as shown, from 8g of Orange Sugar Dough divided equally in two. (They are much smaller than for the geese.)

5. To make all the beaks, you will need 4g of Orange Sugar Dough. Make a small cone shape, slit with a sharp knife, then round off the edges with your finger. Push a small piece of dry spaghetti into the end and secure to the face in-between the cheeks.

6. Make the eyes from two tiny oval shapes of White Sugar Dough. Paint on the pupil with a fine brush and SK Blackberry Paste Food Colour. If the eyes are shut, paint on with diluted SK Blackberry Paste Food Colour.

7. Brush the ducks with SK Confectioners' Glaze, if desired. This helps to bring out their colour so they stand out more.

## Suitcase

1. Mix together 60g of White Sugar Dough with a little Black to make grey. Roll out and cut two oval shapes 5cm across, one for the base and one for the lid. Cut a strip to go around the sides measuring 15cm x 3cm. Glue around the base and join the seam neatly at the back. Set aside to dry.

2. Take the second oval for the lid and cut another strip to go around it measuring 15cm x 1cm. Glue the strip in place and set aside to dry.

3. Make two clasps from White Sugar Dough, each measuring 0.5cm x 1cm. Glue to the case. Make a small fasten for the top clasp and glue into place.

4. Position the dry case on the board at the back of the cake and glue the lid to the side of the cake. Apply a coat of SK Gildesol to the clasps and dust with SK Brilliant Gold Metallic Lustre Dust.

5. Make an assortment of clothes from oddments to fill the case using the pictures as a guide. Glue them to the case and board.

# Materials

20.5cm (8") round cake

Sugar Dough in following amounts:

260g (9oz) Black

95g (3¼oz) Brown

30g (1oz) Green

4g (⅛oz) Peach

30g (1oz) Red

1.74kg (3lb 13oz) White

70g (2½oz) Yellow

Small amounts of Blackberry and White SK Sugar Florist Paste (SFP)

SK Paste Food Colours: Berberis, Bulrush, Chestnut, Holly Ivy, Hyacinth, Leaf Green, Poinsettia and Rose

SK Metallic Lustre Dust: Silver

SK Edible Glue

SK Confectioners' Glaze

SK Glaze Cleaner

Raw spaghetti

# Equipment

36cm x 30cm (14" x 12") oval cake drum

Non-stick board

Large and small rolling pins

Sharp knife

PME modelling tool: scallop and comb tool

Dresden tool

Sugar shaper

Cutting wheel

Design wheel

2cm (¾") round cutter

6cm x 5cm (2⅜" x 2") oval cutter

PME blossom plunger cutter

Small leaf cutter

Medium and fine paintbrushes

Cocktail stick

2 table forks

Olive ribbon to trim

# Grandma's Garden

### Of all the flowers in the garden, Grandma is the fairest rose!

## Covering the Cake and Board

1. Colour 1.1kg of White Sugar Dough with SK Leaf Green Paste Food Colour. Cut off 500g, roll out and cover the cake drum.

2. Cover the cake using the remaining Leaf Green coloured Sugar Dough. Place the cake centrally on the board.

## Apple Tree

1. Take 100g of White Sugar Dough and divide in half. Colour one half with SK Berberis Paste Food Colour and the other with SK Chestnut. Mix the two colours together to create a marbled effect. Cut off 70g of the brown paste for the apple tree and set the remainder to one side. Roll into a cone shape approximately 13cm long, then carefully twist the paste. Take a sharp knife and cut out the branches, as shown. Carefully pull out and round off the edges of the branches, then twist these as well. Mark with a Dresden tool. Push the end of a large paintbrush into the trunk to make a knot. Finally, using a medium paintbrush, paint with diluted SK Bulrush Paste Food Colour.

2. Position the tree on the side of the cake. Glue the base of the tree onto the board 3.5cm from the side of the cake. Arrange the branches over the

side and top and secure with SK Edible Glue.

3. For all the foliage, colour 115g of White Sugar Dough with SK Holly Ivy Paste Food Colour. Use 70g for the leaves and set the remainder to one side. Roll out thinly then cut out lots of leaves using a small leaf cutter. Arrange fifteen in a cluster at the top of each branch.

4. For the apples, divide 25g of Red Sugar Dough into nine pieces and roll each one into a ball. Glue seven apples onto the tree and two onto the board using SK Edible Glue. Make a hole in each apple with the end of a strand of raw spaghetti, then make two tiny leaves from Green Sugar Dough for each apple and glue inside the hole.

# Vine

Twist some of the remaining brown coloured Sugar Dough into a narrow trunk and two branches, then make additional small branches. Cut out twenty five leaves from the Holly Ivy coloured Sugar Dough. Position the vine at the back of the cake and add the leaves, securing in place with SK Edible Glue.

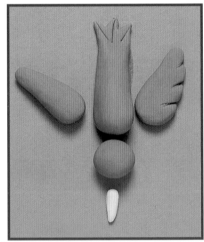

# Bluebirds

Colour 25g of White Sugar Dough with SK Hyacinth Paste Food Colour and divide into five equal pieces. Make a small cone shape for each body, then flatten a tail with your finger. Using the small leaf cutter, cut two 'V' shapes in the tail and round off. Tilt the tail upwards. Roll a small ball for each head and secure with SK Edible Glue. Mark the eyes with raw spaghetti. Make the beaks from tiny pieces of Yellow Sugar Dough and secure with SK Edible Glue. Make the wings from two small cone shapes of blue paste, mark the feathers with the back of a knife and secure to the sides of the body. Place three birds on the vine and two on the tree.

# Birdhouses

Cut out the templates for the birdhouses (page 109) from thin card. Using a small amount of SK Berberis coloured Sugar Dough and any leftover brown coloured Sugar Dough, make all the pieces, attach together with SK Edible Glue and allow to firm before attaching to the side of the cake.

# Fence and Sunflowers

1. Roll out 60g of White Sugar Dough and cut out a rectangle 9.5cm x 6cm. Cut into four strips each 1.5cm wide. Trim to a point at the top and glue in a row to the side of the cake (opposite the apple tree).

2. Roll out a narrow strip of SK Holly Ivy coloured Sugar Dough for the flower stems. Place a length of dry spaghetti in the centre, brush with SK Edible Glue and roll into a very thin flower stem.

3. To make the sunflowers, roll out 40g of Yellow Sugar Dough and cut out three 2cm circles. Place the flower stem on top of the circle and secure with SK Edible Glue. Cut out the flower petals using a small leaf cutter and arrange a layer around the edge of the circle. Place a second row on top and in-between the first row.

4. Take a small ball of Brown Sugar Dough and divide into three. Roll each piece into a ball for the flower centres, then flatten slightly between your fingers. Attach in place in the centre of each flower, then prick it all over with a cocktail stick and leave to dry flat. When dry, stand upright and glue to the fence, then add two more leaves to each stem, as shown.

 # Grass and Small Flowers

Fill a sugar shaper with Green Sugar Dough and extrude short lengths for the grass. Cut off with a knife and place some at the base of the vine, tree and fence, securing with SK Edible Glue. Thinly roll out some Yellow Sugar Dough and cut out the flowers using a PME blossom plunger cutter. Arrange in the grass.

# Basket

1. Roll out 90g of Brown Sugar Dough and cut out the base using an oval cookie cutter. Re-roll the remaining paste to a thickness of 0.5cm for the sides and cut a strip measuring 17.5cm x 4cm. Using two forks, pinch the Sugar Dough together in vertical lines. Repeat all the way across this side piece.

2. Glue the side piece to the base, making a neat join. Roll two thin sausage shapes of Brown Sugar Dough and twist them together to make a rope edge, then glue to the top of the basket. Allow to dry.

3. Make the handle using the same method, but make it thicker. Leave to dry in a curved shape. Attach this to the basket once it has been filled.

# Wool, Knitting and Needles

1. For the blue balls of wool, colour 50g of White Sugar Dough with SK Hyacinth Paste Food Colour, divide in half and place one piece aside. Divide the paste in half again and roll one half into a ball. Add a little white vegetable fat into the second half, place into a sugar shaper with a fine hole disc and extrude the

45

wool strands. Cover the ball with the wool. Make a second ball of blue wool in the same way using the remaining paste.

2. Take 25g of Yellow Sugar Dough and make another ball of wool, as before. Make a small ball of wool using 15g of Green Sugar Dough.

3. For Grandma's knitting, roll out a piece of SK Hyacinth coloured Sugar Dough and cut out a 2.5cm square. Using a PME comb modelling tool, make stitch marks all over the square.

4. To make the knitting needles, roll a thin strip of grey Sugar Dough around a piece of raw spaghetti, in the same way as for the sunflower stems. Add a small flattened ball at one end and roll to a point at the other. Glue the knitting to one needle.

# Cats

1. You will need 250g of Black Sugar Dough, 40g of White Sugar Dough and a small amount of Rose coloured Sugar Dough to complete all the cats. For the body, roll 30g of Black Sugar Dough into a cone shape. For the back legs divide 10g in half and make two more cone shapes, then bend in slightly towards the body.

2. For the front paws, roll 10g of Black Sugar Dough into a sausage shape 6.5cm long and cut in half. For the front claws, roll three tiny cone shapes for each paw and glue in place. For the back paws, roll a small ball and mark with the back of a knife. Roll a thin cone shape for the tail, narrowing at the tip. Add a White Sugar Dough tip on the end.

3. Roll another 10g of Black Sugar Dough into a ball for the head. Make two tiny triangle shapes for the ears, secure in place and fill with smaller triangles of pink on the inside.

4. To make the muzzle, flatten a ball of White Sugar Dough and stick it onto the head. Mark the centre halfway down with the back of a knife. Indent a smile using a PME scallop modelling tool or a small circle cutter. Using the end of a paintbrush, bring down the mouth between the smile. Stick two small balls of White Sugar Dough just above and either side of the muzzle for the eyes and attach a black pupil over the top. Make a pink nose and tongue and fix into place. If you wish to put more white features on the face and body, just make a flattened cone shape, mark with a knife and secure in place.

5. Make two more cats in the same way. Secure two of the cats to the board.

## Maisie's Handy Hints

If the cat is holding a ball of wool, place the wool into position before sticking on the legs and paws.

# Filling the Basket

1. Place one of the cats on its back in the basket. Put the small green ball of wool at the other end. Glue a ball of blue wool to the cat's body and wrap the legs around it. Stick the tail onto the body and over the ball of wool.

2. Make two red knitting needles in the same way as before and push into the ball of green wool. Roll a small, soft piece of Brown Sugar Dough for the basket handle to rest on and glue into position over the top. The handle may need to be supported with foam until it has dried.

# Ladybirds

Take 8g of Red Sugar Dough and roll three small oval shapes. Mark a line down the centre of each with the back of a knife. Roll three small heads from Black Sugar Dough and glue to each body. Make tiny eyes from balls of White Sugar Dough and secure to the heads. To make the legs, take a small amount of Black SFP, roll out a sausage as thinly as you can and cut into short lengths. Brush some SK Edible Glue onto the side of the bug and, using a paintbrush, carefully pick up each leg and press onto the body. Arch the legs and allow to dry. Place in position once they are dry.

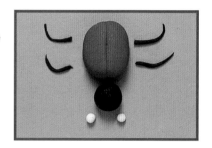

# Grandma's Body and Back Panel of Skirt

1. Colour 125g of White Sugar Dough with SK Rose Paste Food Colour. Cut off 30g for the body and roll into a smooth oval shape.

2. Roll out 15g of the Rose coloured paste and cut out the template for the back of the skirt (see page 109). Position this on top of the cake where Grandma will sit. Place the body in the centre of the panel, then bring the back edge of the panel up to waist height at the back of the body and secure. (This will look as if she is sitting on the skirt.)

# Legs and Shoes

1. To make the legs, add a little Black Sugar Dough to 25g of White to make a pale grey shade. Roll 15g into a sausage shape 12cm long and cut in half. Make a diagonal cut at the top of each leg. To make the shoes, divide 8g of Black Sugar Dough in two and roll each piece into an oval shape. Using a small amount of grey paste, cut out two small circles and place these on top of the shoes. Stick the shoes to the end of the legs, then roll a small strip to go around the ankle and add a button to finish.

2. Cross the legs at the ankles and stick to the body on top of the skirt panel. Support underneath the feet with foam until dry.

# Petticoat Frill and Skirt

1. Roll out 20g of White Sugar Dough into a strip measuring 15cm x 3cm for the petticoat. Make a straight edge using a cutting wheel. Using a design wheel, run a wavy edge along the other. Make a row of dots along the wavy edge and a row above using the end of a piece of raw spaghetti, as shown. Gather gently on the straight edge and glue over the legs in a curved shape.

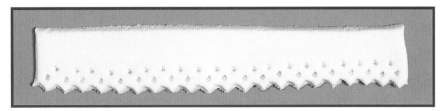

2. To make the skirt, roll out 40g of the Rose coloured paste and cut a curved strip using the template (page 109). Roll out some paler pink paste very thinly and cut out a number of flowers using a blossom plunger cutter. Roll the flowers on to the skirt with a small rolling pin to create a floral pattern. Gather the skirt at the waist and arrange over the petticoat, finishing neatly at the sides and waist. Turn under any 'raw' edges at the sides.

# Apron

Colour 10g of White Sugar Dough with SK Berberis Paste Food Colour. Roll out and cut out the apron template (page 109). Run a design wheel around three sides to make stitch marks, then add a small square pocket. Glue the apron to the waist. Cut out a narrow waistband and secure in place, crossing the ends over at the back.

# Arms and Collar

Roll 12g of Rose coloured paste into a long sausage shape measuring 10cm, make a diagonal cut in the centre and glue to the shoulders. Bring the arms forward to the front of the body. Cut a narrow strip of the same paste for the cuffs, frill using a cocktail stick, cut in half and secure at the wrists. Cut out two small circles for the collar and place them side by side on top of the body.

# Shawl

Using the template (page 109) as a guide, cut out the shape of the shawl from 25g of Yellow Sugar Dough. Run a design wheel in a criss-cross stitch design and fringe the edge using a sharp knife. Place the shawl around the body and cross over at the front.

# Hands and Head

1. Add a little Peach Sugar Dough to 30g of White Sugar Dough to create a pale flesh colour. Make two hands using 5g of the flesh coloured paste. Divide equally, cut to shape and attach to the wrists. Secure the knitting into the hands. Drape a strand of wool over the knitting and down onto the nearest cat lying on the board.

2. Use 25g for the head and roll into a smooth ball. Push a small piece of dry spaghetti down into the body and slide the head over the top. Add the facial features and pull the nose out slightly more than usual to support the glasses. Make two tiny teardrop shapes for the ears and add two small balls in red for earrings. Mark a smile using the edge of a small circle cutter.

3. Paint on the eyebrows and eyelashes using diluted SK Bulrush Paste Food Colour, then paint the lips using SK Poinsettia Paste Food Colour.

# Hair

Fill the sugar shaper with grey Sugar Dough and extrude strands of hair. Start layering at the front parting and go around to the back of the head. Repeat on the other side. Top with a small, round piece of paste covered with strands of hair. Add three small yellow blossoms down the back of the head.

# Spectacles

Take a tiny amount of White SFP and roll it as thinly as you can into a strip approximately 4cm long. Bring both ends up almost into the centre, leaving a small gap, and glue the ends neatly to make a round shape. Place over Grandma's nose and glue into place.

# Finishing Touches

1. Using SK Confectioners' Glaze, paint the cats and other objects on the cake to highlight them.

2. Add SK Glaze Cleaner (or clear alcohol) to SK Silver Metallic Lustre Dust and paint Grandma's hair and spectacles.

# Dish of the Day!

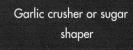

This cheeky Italian chef is in his element! A great celebration cake for chefs and food lovers everywhere.

## Covering the Cake and Board

1. Cover the board using 290g of White Sugar Dough.

2. Using a sharp, serrated knife cut down from the top of the cake to the base to create sloping sides. Once you have the required shape, cover the cake using 290g White Sugar Dough. Position the cake in the centre of the board and allow to firm.

## Spaghetti

Colour 300g of White Sugar Dough with SK Berberis Paste Food Colour. Roll out and cut into long strips using a cutting wheel. Arrange the spaghetti around the sides and on top of the cake and secure. Put a few pieces of spaghetti aside to be added later.

## Tomato

For the sliced tomato, take 110g of Red Sugar Dough, roll into a thick sausage shape and shave off thick pieces with a sharp knife. Scatter on top of the cake and secure with SK Edible Glue.

## Meatballs

Colour 135g of White Sugar Dough with SK Chestnut Paste Food Colour. Roll the paste into six balls then prick each one with a fork to roughen the surface. Place them around the top of the cake, leaving a space in the centre for the chef.

# Chef

1. Add a little Peach Sugar Dough to 45g of White Sugar Dough to create a flesh colour. Take off half the paste for the head and roll into a pear shape, keeping the wider end for the chin. Mark a double chin with the back of a knife at the base, then add the ears and facial features. To make the nose, roll a small amount of flesh paste into a cone shape and pinch in slightly to shape, then glue in place. Mark the eyes using the end of a paintbrush, fill the holes with White Sugar Dough and add a tiny black pupil in each. Create the mouth by marking the upper and lower lips first with a PME scallop tool then, using the end of a paintbrush, push into the mouth to hollow it out. Using diluted SK Poinsettia Paste Food Colour, paint inside the mouth and add a blush to the cheeks.

2. Extrude a little softened Black Sugar Dough through a sugar shaper or garlic crusher for the hair and lay in a short line over the top of each ear. Model two teardrop shapes of Black Sugar Dough for the moustache and glue underneath the nose, twisting the ends a little. Add two tiny teardrop shapes for the eyebrows.

3. For the chef's body, roll 30g of Blue Sugar Dough into a sausage shape. Pinch in at the top making it higher for the neck. Push a piece of dry spaghetti into the body leaving a little showing to support the head. Place the body into the centre of the cake and gently slide the head over the spaghetti, securing with SK Edible Glue.

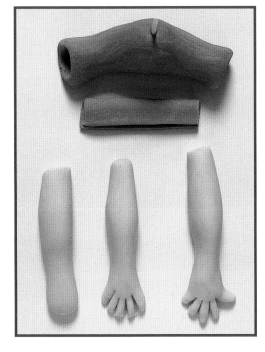

4. To make the upper arms, roll 20g of Blue Sugar Dough into a sausage shape 7cm long and make a diagonal cut in the centre. Glue to either side of the body. Hollow out the end of the upper arm using a scalloped tool so that the lower arm will fit into it.

5. For the lower arms and hands divide the remaining 20g or so of the flesh coloured Sugar Dough in half. Roll each piece into a sausage shape, then narrow at the wrist. Press the hand slightly flat and cut all the digits using a small sharp knife. Press into the palm with a PME ball tool to round off the hand and bend it into position. Glue into the hollow made in the upper arm while the paste is still soft, supporting with foam if necessary until dry. Cut two small strips of Blue Sugar Dough for the shirt cuff measuring 2cm x 6cm and fold in half loosely. Glue over the upper and lower arms to hide the joins.

## Chef's Hat

Using 25g of White Sugar Dough, make a fat cone shape, then make a straight edge at the base and push a small stick of dry spaghetti into it. Add a band and glue around the base. Push the dry spaghetti carefully into the top of the chef's head and secure with SK Edible Glue to hold the hat on firmly. Support the head with foam from the back if necessary until dry.

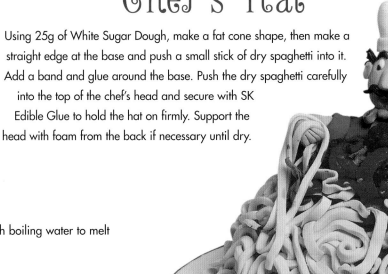

## Finishing Touches

1. Make a few tarragon leaves from Green Sugar Dough.

2. Make some tomato sauce by mixing one tablespoon of icing sugar with just enough boiling water to melt the sugar. Add some SK Poppy Paste Food Colour and drizzle over the meatballs.

3. Finally, add a few strips of spaghetti over the chef's hands.

## Materials

15cm (6") square cake

SK Sugar Dough in following amounts:

Small amount Black

4g ($^1/_8$oz) Brown

1.2kg (2lb 10oz) Peach

850g (1lb 14oz) White

SK Paste Food Colours: Berberis, Blackberry, Fuchsia, Hyacinth, Teddy Bear Brown

SK Edible Glue

Raw spaghetti

## Equipment

28cm (11") hexagonal cake drum

Non-stick board

Large and small rolling pins

Sharp knife

PME modelling tools: scallop and comb tool, flower and leaf shaper tool

Dresden tool

Garlic crusher or sugar shaper

Cutting wheel

2cm ($^3/_4$") round cutter

Fine and medium paintbrushes

Deep orange ribbon to trim

I was inspired to create this design by my Old English Sheepdogs, Misty, Foggy and Sunshine. Sugar Dough really comes into its own with this cake as you need to sculpt as well as model the figures. I have painted the fur on the dogs to create a more realistic effect.

## Covering the Cake and Board

1. Knead a little white vegetable fat into the Peach Sugar Dough until smooth. Take off 600g to cover the board in the usual way.

2. Set a little aside, then use the remaining Peach Sugar Dough to cover the cake. Position in the centre of the cake drum and secure with a little SK Edible Glue.

## Dog on Cake

1. You will need 210g of White Sugar Dough for the dog. Cut off 125g for the body and roll into an oval shape. Make a clean cut at one end using a sharp knife to divide the paste for the front legs. Smooth the edges with your fingers and separate, as shown overleaf.

2. Place the body into position on the top of the cake, then using a PME flower and leaf shaper tool, mark all over to make the coat, keeping the lines flowing naturally downwards. For the head, take off another 50g and roll into a smooth ball, then into a cone shape. Flatten at the front and narrow the snout. Attach the head to the body using a small stick of dry spaghetti for support.

3. Mark the front of the snout in the centre with the back of a knife, then mark the mouth with two short lines on either side. Dilute a little SK Blackberry Paste Food Colour in a little cooled

53

boiled water and paint an outline on the mouth using a fine paintbrush. Make two holes for the eyes using the end of a piece of raw spaghetti. Roll a small ball of Black Sugar Dough for the nose and insert two tiny balls of Black into the eye sockets. Make two small cone shapes for the ears and mark with a PME flower and leaf shaper modelling tool.

4.   Use the remaining Sugar Dough for the

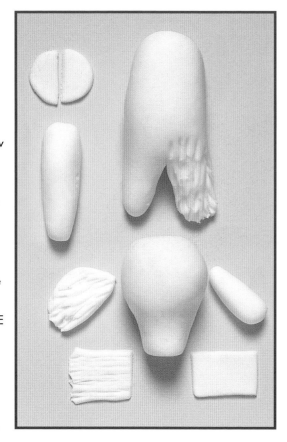

fur trimmings. Add more fur under the chin, at the back of the head and add a fringe on the top. Exact measurements are not important here, as all you need to do is keep adding small pieces of flattened Sugar Dough and marking with the modelling tool, building up the shape until you have the desired result. Secure all the parts with SK Edible Glue. Once the dog is complete, paint him with diluted SK Blackberry Paste Food Colour using a medium paintbrush.

# Girl

1.   For the body, use 80g of White Sugar Dough, shape this into an oval and then into a reversed 'S' shape. Taper the paste at the top for the neck and push a small piece of dry spaghetti into the centre to support the head. Use a Dresden tool to model the creases in the apron and skirt.

2.   Make the arms using 20g of White Sugar Dough equally divided in two. Roll each piece into a cone shape and mark the cuffs and creases as before. For the hands, mix a tiny piece of White Sugar Dough with Peach Sugar Dough to make a flesh colour, then divide equally. Make the hands in the usual way then attach to the wrist of each arm and bend the right arm at the elbow so that it will rest on top of the dog.

3.   For the boots, divide a tiny piece of White Sugar Dough into two equal pieces, then roll each one into a ball and then into a cone shape. Flatten the thickest end to make the sole, as shown, and secure to the body. Paint with diluted SK Blackberry Paste Food Colour.

4.   To make the collar, roll out some White Sugar Dough and cut out a 2cm diameter circle. Cut in half and attach in place with SK Edible Glue.

5.   Position the girl next to the dog on top of the cake and place her right arm over the dog's back. Add a bow made from White Sugar Dough at the back of the apron.

6.   For the head you will need 15g of White Sugar Dough mixed with a little Peach Sugar Dough to make a flesh colour. Roll into a smooth ball and gently slide over the dry spaghetti at the neck. Mark the nose in the centre of the face and fill with a tiny cone shape of flesh coloured paste. Make two small cone shapes for the ears and mark the inside with the end of a paintbrush. Mark the eyes just above and either side of the nose, then fill with tiny balls of Brown Sugar Dough. Mark the smile with a scallop modelling tool. Blush

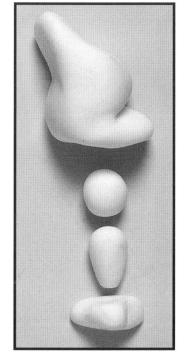

the cheeks with watered down SK Fuchsia Paste Food Colour and outline the smile with a fine paintbrush using the same colour.

7. For the hair, colour 20g of White Sugar Dough with SK Teddy Bear Brown Paste Food Colour. If necessary, soften the paste slightly with a little white vegetable fat, fill the cup of a garlic crusher or a sugar shaper with the paste and extrude strands for the hair. Arrange around the head and secure with SK Edible Glue. To make the curls at the top, simply twist a couple of strands together. (This will hide any joints at the top of the head.)

8. Paint the dress with diluted SK Fuchsia Paste Food Colour, keeping the colour darker around the collar.

# Sitting and Lying Puppies

1. For each small puppy you will need approximately 35g of White Sugar Dough. To make the sitting puppies, take off 15g for the body and roll into a cone shape. Using a sharp knife, make a horizontal cut halfway through the centre, then make a vertical cut half way down at the thickest end to divide the legs. Pull each leg out slightly and smooth the edges, as shown opposite.

2. Push a small piece of dry spaghetti into the neck. Using a Dresden tool, mark the fur. Add small flat pieces of paste to the chest and paws to build up the required shape, continually marking with the Dresden tool.

3. For the head, roll 8g of White Sugar Dough into a cone shape and make as described for the larger dog. Where a tongue is added, push the end of a paintbrush into the mouth area, make a small oval shape with a tiny amount of pink coloured Sugar Dough, dab a little SK Edible Glue into the mouth and push the tongue into the hole. Mark down the centre of the tongue with the back of a knife (this will hold the tongue firmly in place). You can create a range of expressions on the puppies' faces, which will give your cake real character.

4. Make the lying down puppies in the same way, but construct the body and legs separately, as shown opposite. Attach all the puppies in place on the board.

# Boy

1. Colour 40g of White Sugar Dough with SK Hyacinth Paste Food Colour. Take off 30g for the body and roll into an oval shape.

2. Take 55g of White Sugar Dough and tint with a little Peach Sugar Dough to make a flesh colour. Take off 20g for the legs. Roll into a sausage shape measuring 10cm and cut in half.

3. For the trousers, colour 45g of White Sugar Dough with SK Teddy Bear Brown Paste Food Colour, take off 15g and set the rest aside. Roll out a strip measuring 7cm x 3cm and

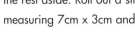

56

wrap around the lower half of the body. Place the body in an upright position and secure to the cake.

4. Roll out another strip of the same size in the same colour, cut in half and make a diagonal cut at the top, as shown. Wrap each piece around the top half of the legs, then glue the legs to the body in a bent position.

5. For the arms, roll 15g of flesh coloured paste into a sausage shape and divide in half. Cut a strip from 10g of the Hyacinth coloured Sugar Dough and cover the top of the arms in the same way as for the legs. Cut out a thumb and four fingers and round off. Secure the right arm only to the body and place the left arm to one side.

6. For the shoes divide 4g of Brown Sugar Dough in half and roll both pieces into an oval shape. Mark the sole with the back of a knife and cut a small fringed square for the front of the shoe. Secure to the legs with SK Edible Glue.

7. Make the head using 20g of flesh coloured Sugar Dough. Follow the same method as for the girl but make the nose and ears slightly larger. Paint his hair using SK Teddy Bear Brown Paste Food Colour and a fine brush.

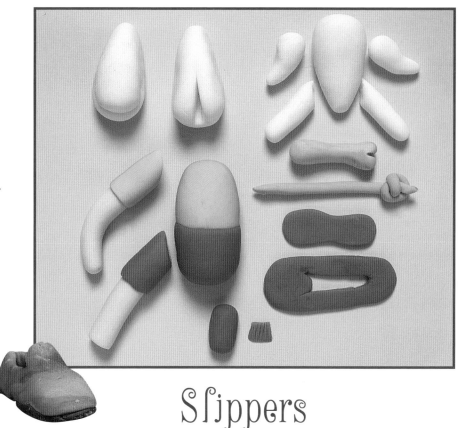

# Puppies with Boy

1. Make the two puppies as before, making their body and legs separately. Attach in place and position their faces so that their tongues are licking the boy's face.

2. Place the boy's left arm into position, bringing it around the puppy.

# Dog Bowl

Take 15g of SK Teddy Bear Brown coloured Sugar Dough and roll into a ball. Flatten the top with your finger and smooth the sides straight. To make the biscuits, chop up small pieces of assorted colours you have left over. Paint 'DOG' on the side of the bowl using SK Blackberry Paste Food Colour and a fine brush. Secure in position on the board.

# Chewy Knotted Bone

Roll a thin sausage of SK Berberis coloured Sugar Dough and make a knot in each end by wrapping a piece of paste around and tucking in the ends. Secure in place with SK Edible Glue.

# Slippers

For two slippers you will need 15g of SK Teddy Bear Brown coloured Sugar Dough. Roll a piece into a cigar shape, press flat until it measures 4cm x 1.5cm, then mould into the shape of a sole and narrow in the middle. Cut out another shape of the same colour measuring 6cm x 2cm when flat, then mark the front using a PME scallop tool. Cut a thin strip out of the centre. Fix to the top of the shoe around the sole and glue the finished slippers in place.

# Dog Bone

Take 4g of SK Berberis coloured Sugar Dough and roll into a cigar shape. Narrow slightly in the middle and mark each end with the back of a knife to resemble a bone. Place on top of the cake.

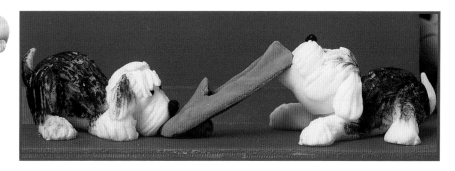

## Materials

25.5cm (10") round cake

SK Sugar Dough in following amounts:

85g (3oz) Blue

80g (2³/₄oz) Brown

510g (1lb 2oz) Green

30g (1oz) Peach

800g (1lb 12oz) White

800g (1lb 12oz) Yellow

SK Paste Food Colours: Blackberry, Bulrush, Chestnut, Holly Ivy, Poppy, Teddy Bear Brown and Terracotta

SK Dust Food Colour: Berberis

SK Edible Glue

SK Confectioners' Glaze

## Equipment

33cm (13") heart shaped cake drum

Non-stick board

Large and small rolling pins

Sharp knife

PME modelling tools: scallop and comb tool, bulbous cone tool

Sugar shaper

4cm and 3cm (1²/₂" and 1¹/₈") round cutters

Fine and medium paintbrushes

Cocktail stick

Fine scissors

Thin card

Foam pieces

Green ribbon to trim

# Piggy Plonk

These naughty pigs are having the time of their lives! Once you have mastered how to model a basic pig, this project is straightforward and great fun to make.

## Covering the Cake and Board

1. Knead 510g of Green Sugar Dough, roll out and cover the cake drum. The pointed end of the drum will go to the back of the cake.

2. To cover the cake, colour 800g of Yellow Sugar Dough with SK Teddy Bear Brown Paste Food Colour to make a golden colour. Roll out and cover the cake. Set aside the excess paste to make the straw.

## Straw

Using the same colour Sugar Dough as the cake, slightly moisten the paste, fill a sugar shaper and extrude strands using the disc with the largest holes. Cut off tufts with a sharp knife and arrange the straw around the cake.

## Wheelbarrow

1. Make the templates from thin card (see page 110). Knead and roll out 80g of Blue Sugar Dough to 0.5cm thickness and cut out the pieces for the bottom and sides. Glue the pieces together using SK Edible Glue mixed with a little Blue Sugar Dough to stiffen. Support the sides with pieces of foam and leave to dry for 24 hours.

2. Make the legs by rolling a sausage shape of Blue Sugar Dough 1cm thick and 7cm long. From this, cut two back legs each 2cm long and two front legs each 1.5cm long. Turn the wheelbarrow upside down and glue the legs into position, then leave to dry for another 24 hours.

### Maisie's Handy Hints

As the wheelbarrow will need to dry hard, it is advisable to make it at least three days in advance.

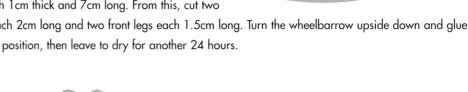

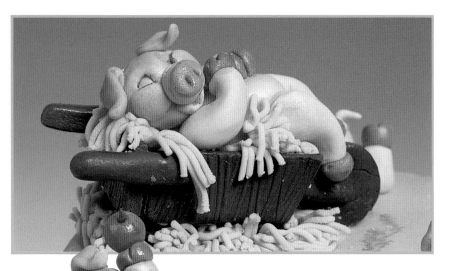

3. For the handle and wheel supports, roll another sausage 1cm thick and 7cm long. Using a sharp knife, cut off one length measuring 4cm and split lengthways for the handles. Split the remaining 3cm lengthways for the wheel support. Glue the flat side of the handle to the wheelbarrow while it is still upside down.

4. Roll out some more Blue Sugar Dough and cut out the wheel with a 3cm round cutter. Sandwich this between the wheel supports and leave to dry before fixing.

5. Finally, place the wheelbarrow on top of the straw. Glue the wheel to the front, supporting with foam until dry. Fill the wheelbarrow with straw for the pig to rest on.

## Cider Barrel

Roll 70g of Brown Sugar Dough into a ball. Using the end of a small rolling pin, hollow out the inside of the barrel by twisting the rolling pin backwards and forwards. Continue to shape the barrel with your fingers until the hole is deep and wide enough to hold the pig. Mark the barrel with a knife to make a wood effect. Place the barrel on top of a 4cm round cutter as this will keep it in shape while it dries.

## Pigs

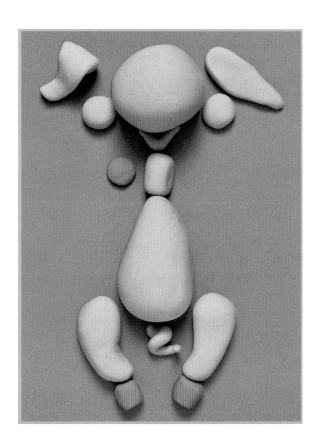

1. Knead together 670g of White Sugar Dough and 30g of Peach Sugar Dough to make a pale pink shade. Take 30g of this and add some SK Terracotta Paste Food Colour to make the trotters for the large pigs. For the piglets' trotters, add a little SK Poinsettia Paste Food Colour.

2. To make a body shape, roll 30g of the pale pink coloured Sugar Dough into a ball and then into a cone shape (the narrow end will be at the top).

3. For each back leg, roll 10g of the coloured Sugar Dough into a cone shape and flatten at the narrowest end. Secure the legs to the body, then place a small ball on the end for the hoof and mark with the back of a knife. For the front legs, roll 8g into a sausage shape. Using a sharp knife, make a diagonal cut across the middle and make a straight cut at each end. Secure the diagonal cut to the body and add a hoof to each as before.

4. Roll 25g into a ball for the head and add the facial features. Make two trianglular shapes for the ears from tiny pieces of Sugar Dough. Glue to the head and bring the pointed end forward. Make the tail from a very thin sausage shape, make it into a curl and secure to the body.

## Maisie's Handy Hints

When you are making the pig in the barrel, put the pointed end of the body inside.

# Cider Flagons

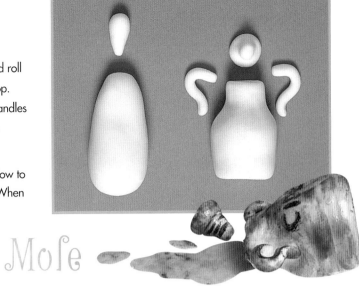

1. To make four cider flagons you will need 100g of White Sugar Dough. Take a quarter of the Sugar Dough and roll into a cone shape. Place on a non-stick board and roll the thick end to create a bottle shape, then flatten the top. Insert the smooth end of PME bulbous cone modelling tool and twist into the neck to hollow it out. Make two handles from thin sausage shapes and attach to either side of the neck. Make a cork from a small cone shape which is flattened on the top.

2. Repeat until you have four flagons, then leave to dry. Paint with diluted SK Chestnut Paste Food Colour and allow to dry. Using a fine paintbrush, paint the name onto each flagon with diluted SK Blackberry Paste Food Colour. When the paint is dry, glue to the cake and board using SK Edible Glue.

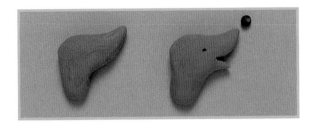

# Mole

1. To make the mole and molehill, you will need 8g of Brown Sugar Dough. Cut off a quarter of the paste for the head and roll into a cone shape, then add a tiny ball at the tip of the nose. Using a pair of fine scissors, snip under the nose to make the mouth, then mark the eyes with the end of a cocktail stick. Glue the mole to the board using SK Edible Glue, then paint the back of the head and nose with SK Blackberry Paste Food Colour.

2. For the hands, take a tiny piece of the paste used for the pigs and divide in half. Roll each piece into a cone shape and mark the fingers with a knife. Carefully round each finger and set aside.

# Molehill

Brush SK Edible Glue around the mole. Crumble a little Brown Sugar Dough and sprinkle the crumbs onto the glue. Place the mole's hands either side of the head and over the top of the crumbs. Secure with SK Edible Glue.

# Apples

Take 30g of White Sugar Dough and divide in half. Colour one half with SK Holly Ivy Paste Food Colour and the other half with SK Poppy. Roll both colours into small balls and make a hole in each with a cocktail stick. Roll small stalks for some of the apples from Brown Sugar Dough and attach with SK Edible Glue. Secure the apples into place.

# Finishing Touches

1. Attach all the pigs, flagons, apples and straw in place with SK Edible Glue.

2. Brush the pigs' ears with SK Berberis Dust Food Colour. Paint the eyes and eyelashes on the pigs using diluted SK Bulrush Paste Food Colour.

3. Glaze the apples, cider barrel, flagons and spilled cider with SK Confectioners' Glaze.

# Gone Fishin'

There's always time for one last bite, as any dedicated fisherman knows! The term 'Bogey' used here comes from an Australian term 'bogey hole' meaning a natural pool in which to swim. However, I think I'd avoid swimming in Bogey Creek!

## Materials

25.5cm x 20cm (10" x 8") oval cake

SK Sugar Dough in following amounts:

10g (just over $^1/_4$oz) Black

175g (6oz) Brown

185g (6$^1/_2$oz) Green

15g ($^1/_2$oz) Peach

45g (1$^1/_2$oz) Red

2.4kg (5lb 4$^1/_2$oz) White

45g (1$^1/_2$oz) Yellow

Small amount of White SK Sugar Florist Paste

SK Paste Food Colours: Blackberry, Chestnut, Hyacinth, Desert Storm, Teddy Bear Brown and Wisteria

SK Dust Food Colours: Gentian, Green Envy, Hyacinth, Marigold and Poppy

SK Moon Beams Lustre Dust Colours: Jade and Topaz

SK Edible Glue

OP White Unbreakable Gel

Clear alcohol

Raw spaghetti

## Equipment

38cm x 33cm (15" x 13") oval cake drum

Non-stick board

Large and small rolling pins

Taffeta veining rolling pin

Craft knife

PME modelling tools: blade and shell tool, scallop and comb tool, flower and leaf shaper tool

Sugar shaper

Posy pic (optional)

4cm and 6cm (1$^1/_2$" and 2$^3/_8$") round cutters

Set of 4 PME rose petal cutters

Medium and fine paintbrushes

Florist wire

Fine scissors

Plastic ruler

Piping bag and no. 3 piping nozzle

Olive ribbon to trim

**IMPORTANT Some of the decorations on this cake contain wires. Ensure these are all removed before the cake is eaten.**

## Covering the Cake and Board

1. Colour 700g of White Sugar Dough with SK Desert Storm Paste Food Colour and cover the board.

2. For the cake you will need 1.2kg of White Sugar Dough. Cut off 150g and mix with SK Hyacinth Paste Food Colour to create pale blue, then take off another 150g and colour a deeper shade of the same colour. Marble the colours together and cover the cake. Put any leftover paste aside. Secure the cake centrally to the board.

## Frieze

1. Colour 100g of White Sugar Dough with SK Hyacinth Paste Food Colour to make a deeper shade of blue for the sky. Roll out and cut out four shapes to go all around the cake using the template (page 110).

2. For the green trees take 50g of Green Sugar Dough and cut out two sizes using the templates (page 110). Cut out the brown trees using SK Teddy Bear Brown coloured Sugar Dough (you could use leftover paste from the boat, as described overleaf). Glue the trees over the join of the frieze, overlapping them from right to left. Finally, put three extra trees in the centre of the skyline where the jetty will be situated.

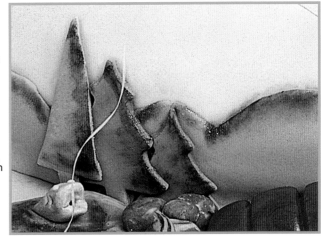

3. Dust all around the edges of the clouds with SK Hyacinth Dust Food Colour using a dry brush. Edge one side of the green trees with SK Green Envy Dust Food Colour.

63

# Flooded Boat

1. For the base of the boat, roll out 150g of the marbled blue Sugar Dough to 2cm thickness and cut out the required shape using the template (page 110). Indent the surface with your finger to make it uneven like water.

2. For the sides of the boat, colour 100g of White Sugar Dough with SK Teddy Bear Brown Paste Food Colour. Cut out an oblong shape measuring 15cm x 6cm, 0.5cm thick. Texture with a taffeta veining rolling pin to give a wood effect, pressing quite hard into the paste to enlarge the piece to 15cm x 9cm. Cut out the shapes for the boat using the templates. Glue these pieces to the base of the boat and leave to dry. Cut out a 2cm triangle and glue to the front.

3. Place the completed boat on top of the cake set at an angle. Attach a thin sausage shape of marbled blue Sugar Dough all around the base of the boat and, using a medium paintbrush, push the paste upwards to resemble rippled water. Make small paper-thin shapes from the paste to resemble spilling water and place over the side and back of the boat.

4. Make two row locks using a small amount of White Sugar Dough. Roll into a small cone shape then cut in the centre of the thick end with a craft knife. Round off the edges and curve, cut a straight edge at the narrow end and glue to each side of the boat, making sure that the one holding the oar is the right way round.

5. To make the oar, roll 10g of the Teddy Bear Brown coloured Sugar Dough into the shape of a baseball bat, as shown. Flatten the end with your finger and gently roll a taffeta veining rolling pin over it. Paint the end with SK Poppy Dust Food Colour mixed with a little alcohol. Leave to firm before securing it into the row lock on the side of the boat.

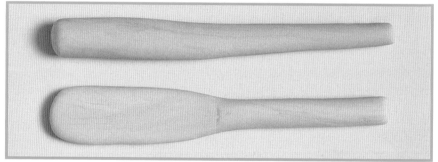

# Fisherman

1. Colour 30g of White Sugar Dough with SK Wisteria Paste Food Colour. Cut off 15g for the body and roll into a cone shape. Place inside the boat towards the back, leaning slightly forward. Push a stick of dry spaghetti down the centre to support the head.

2. Use some of the remaining blue paste for the legs and roll into a sausage shape 9cm long. Make a diagonal cut in the centre and a straight cut at each end. Attach the legs to the body, bending at the knees and keeping them apart. Bring the lower legs forward as if they are submerged in the water.

3. Roll out 4g of Red Sugar Dough and cut a strip measuring 6cm x 1cm. Place this below the waistline at the back of the body to resemble a shirt that will show beneath the jacket.

4. For the jacket, colour 40g of Green Sugar Dough with SK Desert Storm Paste Food Colour to make a khaki shade. Using the template (page 110), cut out the jacket. Turn under the lower edge to make a loose fold, then bring the edges together at the front and neaten at the neck.

5. Roll 10g of the same paste into a sausage shape for the arms, make a diagonal cut in the centre and a straight cut at each end. Secure to the shoulders and bend at the elbows. Support with foam until dry if necessary.

6. Make up 40g of flesh paste by adding a little Peach Sugar Dough to White. Take off 10g for the head and roll into a teardrop shape. Slide over the spaghetti at the neck and secure with SK Edible Glue. Add the facial features, as shown. (I have given him a large nose so that it will not be lost under the hat.)

7. Fill a sugar shaper with 4g of softened Brown Sugar Dough and extrude strands for the hair. Secure onto the head.

8. For the jacket hood, roll 4g of khaki coloured paste into a small cigar shape 5cm long, taper at each end and attach to the jacket. Using a PME flower and leaf shaper modelling tool, mark some creases in the hood. Make a small collar from a strip of Red Sugar Dough measuring 4cm x 1cm, cut in half and glue under the chin.

9. For the hat, roll out 8g and cut out a 4cm circle. Round off the edges, place over the head and shape as shown. For the crown, roll a small ball of the remaining Sugar Dough, flatten between your thumb and finger, then make a dip in the centre so that it will hold some water. Fill with a little blue paste and add a few raindrops on the brim of the hat. Paint some dark green blotches over the coat and hat using SK Green Envy Dust Food Colour mixed with clear alcohol.

# Fishing Rod

1. Cut a 17cm length of florist wire and make a curve at one end. Make the reel from pieces of Black, grey and SK Teddy Bear Brown coloured Sugar Dough secured together in a sausage shape. Slide the wire through all these pieces and secure together using SK Edible Glue. Roll a tiny strip of White Sugar Dough for the brake and attach to the front of the reel.

2. Roll a very thin strip of White SFP 0.5cm long, join the ends and add a straight piece over the join to strengthen, as shown. Allow to firm, then thread them onto the wire and secure with SK Edible Glue. Push the end of the wire into the boat, ensuring it does not penetrate the cake, or use a posy pic (as described in "Let's Party", pages 22-25). Make a small 'S' shaped hook from SFP to go through the back of the boy's trousers. Leave to dry.

3. Make the hands from 4g of flesh coloured paste. Glue the right hand to the arm and face and wrap the fingers of the left hand around the fishing rod.

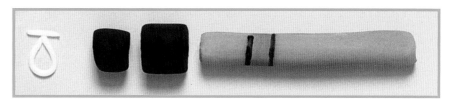

Finally, add two narrow strips of Red for the shirt cuffs.

4. To make the fishing line, make up the Unbreakable Gel following the instructions on the packet and allow to stand for four hours. Place into a piping bag with a no. 3 nozzle and pipe a long wavy line onto a non-stick board or onto acetate. Remember that the gel will need to be long enough to go from the reel down to the hook at the back of the boy. When dry, carefully remove from the board or acetate and place to one side. Repeat the same method for the camper's fishing line.

# Dog

Colour 15g of White Sugar Dough with SK Teddy Bear Brown Paste Food Colour. Make two paws from small sausage shapes marked with the back of a knife and glue them to the side of the boat. Roll the head and place in-between the paws. Mark the centre of the face with the back of a knife then mark the mouth with a PME scallop modelling tool. Cut out two cheeks using a small PME rose petal cutter. Cut off the point to make a straight edge, then place them edge to edge down the centre of the face. Add eyes, a nose and a small tongue. Make cone shapes for the ears and glue to the sides of the head.

# Floating Objects

1. The radio is made from 10g of White Sugar Dough mixed with a little Black to make grey. Cut an oblong measuring 2.5cm x 2cm, 0.5cm thick. Make a diagonal cut at the bottom. Roll a thin sausage shape for the handle and bend to shape. Cut a dial from White Sugar Dough and roll a thin strip for the ariel. Secure with SK Edible Glue. Paint the dial with SK Blackberry Paste Food Colour. Position the radio inside the front of the boat.

2. The other objects each require approximately 4g of the appropriate coloured Sugar Dough. Make two cola cans, red floats, a bone, a slice of bread and an apple and secure them all to the top of the cake.

3. Dust around all the objects with SK Hyacinth Dust Food Colour.

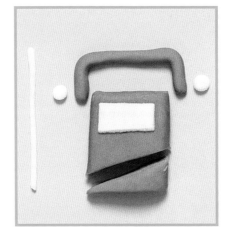

# Fish

The fish on the top of the cake are made from 8g of grey paste. Roll a cone shape 6cm long, flatten the tail, then cut a 'V' shape into it and mark with the back of a knife. Indent the mouth with the flat end of a rose petal cutter, then open it up with the bristles of a small paintbrush. Using scallop modelling tool, mark the gills and scales. Finally, add a yellow eye. Cut the fish in half, putting the tail end up at the back of the boat and the head on top of the cake. Dust around the fish as before.

# Foliage and Bulrushes

Make the foliage and bulrushes in the same way as in "Ducks Keep Out!" (pages 84-88) Position the foliage first, then push the bulrushes into the thickest part so that the wires do not penetrate the cake, or use a posy pic.

# Ducks

## Maisie's Handy Hints

Remember when painting to leave everything to dry before reapplying any paint. If you go over the surface again when it is wet, it will lift off the paint you have already applied.

1. Make two ducks using 8g of White Sugar Dough for each. Take off 4g for each body, mould into a cone shape, then mould the neck and head, as shown. Make a small cone shape of Yellow Sugar Dough for the beak, then split with a craft knife and round off the edges. Cut off the point and secure to the head. Make wings for each duck (these are the same shape as the body but much smaller) then mark the feathers with the back of a knife. Add a tiny yellow eye.

2. Paint the ducks using SK Dust Food Colours mixed with clear alcohol and a fine brush. Paint the body with Bulrush, the head with Green Envy and the wings with Gentian. When the ducks are completely dry, dust over the heads with SK Jade Moon Beams.

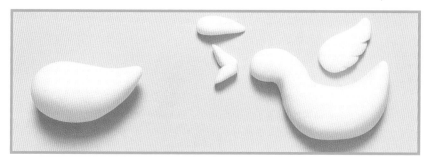

# Jetty

1. Roll out 80g of Brown Sugar Dough to 0.5cm thickness. Run a veining rolling pin over the surface, pressing quite hard. Cut out two rectangles measuring 5.5cm x 3.5cm. Mark vertical lines with the edge of a ruler to resemble planks. Glue one piece on top of the other with the plain sides together. Cut out two side strips using the template (page 110) and glue to the front and back of the other piece.

2. Knead the remaining Brown Sugar Dough, roll out a sausage shape 1cm thick and 6cm long and cut into four for the legs. Glue the legs to each corner, pushing a short piece of dry spaghetti down into the centre of each one (leaving none showing at the top). Set aside to dry, then position on the board and secure with SK Edible Glue.

# Boy on Jetty

1. For the body, roll 15g of Yellow Sugar Dough into a cone shape and push a piece of raw spaghetti through the middle. Colour 40g of White Sugar Dough with SK Hyacinth Paste Food Colour, cut out a 6cm circle, then lay the body on top of the circle and secure to the front of the body. Bring the sides together and trim off the excess paste with a small pair of scissors.

2. Pull the back away and push a hole in the centre with a piece of raw spaghetti. Insert the 'S' shaped hook into the hole, secure with SK Edible Glue and support with foam until dry. Place the body on top of the jetty leaning over towards the edge of the board.

3. Divide the remaining blue coloured Sugar Dough in half and roll into two cone shapes for the legs. Glue to the sides of the body and bend at the knees. Make the Wellingtons from 15g of Green Sugar Dough divided equally. Roll into two sausage shapes, turn up at the toes, then make a straight cut at the top. Secure the boots to the knees of the trousers.

4. To make the arms, roll 10g of Yellow Sugar Dough into a sausage shape measuring 9cm, cut in half and attach to the body. Support the right arm with foam and push a small piece of dry spaghetti into the end. Place the left arm on the jetty. For the braces, cut two small strips of Red Sugar Dough and make a slit at both ends of each one. Glue into place, crossing over at the back, then finish with two small green buttons on each tab.

5. For the hands and head you will require 15g of flesh coloured Sugar Dough. Take off 8g and roll into a smooth ball for the head. Slide over the spaghetti at the neck and secure, then add the facial expressions. Make the hands and secure in place. Cut two small oblongs of Yellow Sugar Dough for the collar and tuck under the chin.

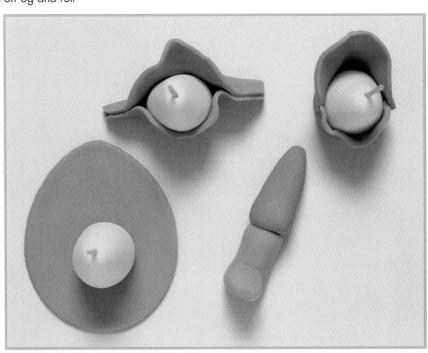

6. To make the hair, colour 8g of White Sugar Dough with SK Teddy Bear Brown Paste Food Colour. Soften the paste and extrude through a sugar shaper, then arrange around the head. Make the hat using 8g of the khaki coloured Sugar Dough as described for the fisherman. Paint with blotches of SK Marigold Dust Food Colour mixed with alcohol.

7. Secure the length of Unbreakable Gel to the 'S' shaped hook at the back of the boy's trousers, thread through the loops of the fishing rod and secure the other end to the reel. Do not pull too tightly or it may break the loops. The dried gel should be fairly pliable so you can bend it to the shape required before threading it through the loops.

# Fishing Bag

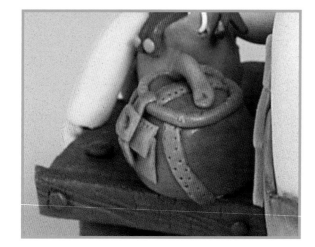

Colour 20g of White Sugar Dough with SK Teddy Bear Brown Paste Food Colour. Roll into a ball then mould to shape, as shown. Colour 4g of White Sugar Dough with SK Chestnut Paste Food Colour and roll a thin strip to go around the top. Secure in place, then make stitch marks with a cocktail stick. Attach a small square shape for the front pocket and a narrower piece for the flap. Run a strip from the top of the bag over the pocket and finish with a small square buckle. Add a small sausage shape for the handle and run a thin strip down each corner. Secure to the jetty with SK Edible Glue.

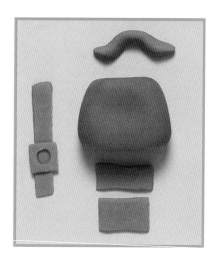

# Camper

1. Roll out 15g of the blue paste left over from the cake and cut out a shape for the pool of water using the template (page 110) as a guide. Place in front of the trees and indent with your fingers.

   Make the sleeping bag from 25g of Red Sugar Dough, then use a PME blade tool to indent lines across it. Make a zip from Yellow Sugar Dough and glue in place. Make a flattened oval shape for the pillow using 10g of Yellow Sugar Dough. Place this at the top of the sleeping bag.

2. Make the collar and arms from Green Sugar Dough, glue the collar in place first then attach the arms either side. Paint on the stripes using SK Green Envy Dust Food Colour mixed with alcohol. Make the head and hands in the usual way and secure in place. Paint the hair onto the back and sides of the head using SK Chestnut Paste Food Colour.

3. Make the hat from 8g of khaki coloured paste as previously described and place over the head and face. Paint of a few blotches with SK Marigold Dust Food Colour. Glue three teardrops for fishing flies onto the hat.

4. Cut a length of florist wire 11cm long, tie a length of unbreakable gel around one end and push the other end through the hand and sleeping bag. Secure the other end of the line with a float.

5. Marble 15g of White Sugar Dough with 4g of Black to make the stones, leaving enough aside to make the head of the fish. Roll the stones into various sizes and place around the sleeping bag. Add some extra foliage using Green Sugar Dough.

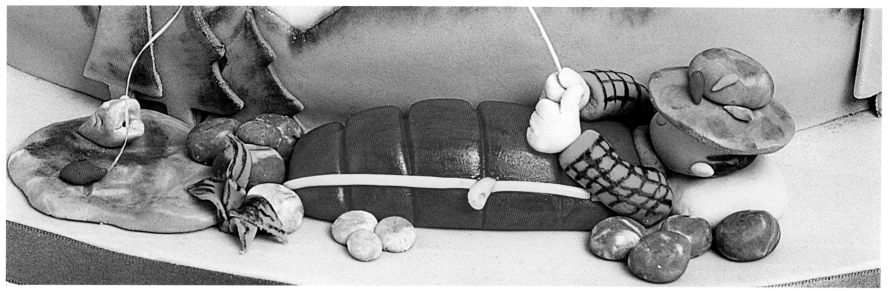

# Bogey Creek

1. Make the sign from 10g of White Sugar Dough coloured with SK Teddy Bear Brown Paste Food Colour. Roll out and cut a strip measuring 6cm x 2cm. Allow to dry, then paint on the name using a fine paintbrush and SK Green Envy Dust Food Colour mixed with clear alcohol.

2. For the post, roll 10g of Brown Sugar Dough into a sausage shape 7cm long and flatten to a width of 1.5cm. Make a straight cut at each end then cut in half. Mark wood grain on each piece with a knife. Push a piece of raw spaghetti down through the centre of each piece, leaving a little showing at the base to push into the water.

3. Lay the post flat and glue on the sign. Add a small ball to each corner and press with the end of some dry spaghetti to resemble nails. Do not stand upright until dry.

4. Using the template (page 110) as a guide, roll out 25g of White Sugar Dough marbled with SK Hyacinth and cut out the shape for the pool of water. Secure to the board, then glue the signpost into position. Push the water around the base of the posts.

5. Make the foliage and bulrushes as previously described and secure around the signpost.

6. Make a frog as described in "Ducks Keep Out!" (page 84-88) using 12g of Green Sugar Dough. Add some markings with SK Green Envy Dust Food Colour mixed with alcohol. Secure the duck in place at the water side.

# Grizzly Bear

You will require 75g of Brown Sugar Dough to make the bear and 4g of White Sugar Dough coloured with Chestnut Paste Food Colour for the snout. Make the bear as described in "Let's Party" (pages 72-75) using 25g for the body, 25g for the legs, 12g for the arms, and 20g for the head and ears. Add the facial features as shown and secure to the board.

# Fish

Divide 10g of Green Sugar Dough in half and make two fish. Take out two bite marks from one using a PME scallop modelling tool. Dust the fish with SK Jade Moon Beams when completed. Make two smaller fish using 4g of grey Sugar Dough equally divided, then dust with SK Topaz Moon Beams. Glue all four fish in place.

## Materials

20.5cm (8") hexagonal cake

SK Sugar Dough in following amounts:

50g (1³/₄oz) Blue

50g (1³/₄oz) Green

65g (2¹/₄oz) Peach

165g (5³/₄oz) Violet

2.34kg (5lb 2¹/₂oz) White

50g (1³/₄oz) Yellow

SK Paste Food Colours: Berberis, Bulrush, Chestnut, Gentian and Poinsettia

SK Metallic Lustre Dust Colour: Snowflake

SK Edible Glue

Raw spaghetti

## Equipment

30.5cm (12") round cake drum

Non-stick board

Rolling pin

Sharp knife

PME modelling tools: blade and shell tool, scallop and comb, bulbous cone tool

Cutting wheel

Garrett frill cutter

Blossom cutter (small)

Sugar shaper

Medium and fine paintbrushes

Narrow pink braid and pink ribbon to trim

# Dance Ballerina, Dance!

This cake was inspired by a photograph of my small granddaughter, resplendent in her ballet costume. This is an ideal design for any budding ballerina!

## Covering the Cake and Board

1. Knead together 400g of White Sugar Dough with 115g of Violet Sugar Dough to create a lilac shade. Roll out the paste on a non-stick board and cover the drum.

2. Knead 900g of White Sugar Dough then colour with a little SK Poinsettia Paste Food Colour to create a pink shade. Cover the cake, then secure it to the centre of the board.

3. Trim the base of the cake with narrow pink braid, attaching in place with SK Edible Glue.

## Swags

1. For each swag, take 40g of White Sugar Dough and roll out thinly. Cut a rectangle 9cm x 13cm and fold lengthways in a concertina fashion. Brush SK Edible Glue down the ends of each strip, then gather the paste together.

2. Brush along the back of each strip with SK Edible Glue, ensuring the ends are covered, then carefully lift the swag and attach to two corners of the cake. Gently push the swag onto the cake to ensure it is secure.

3. Repeat the same method until all six sides have a swag.

# Tails and Bows

1. To make each tail, you will need 30g of White Sugar Dough. Roll the paste out thinly and cut out the tail shape using the template (see page 110). Pinch and cut in the centre.

2. Attach pairs of tails in-between a swag on a corner of the cake. (The join does not have to be neat as it will be covered by a bow.) Repeat the method for making tails until you have two on each corner.

3. To make a bow, take a small amount of White Sugar

Dough, roll out fairly thinly and cut a strip 2cm x 9cm. Apply a little SK Edible Glue to the centre and fold each end over to meet in the middle as shown.

4. Turn the paste over and pinch gently in the centre. Using a PME blade tool, mark the centre. To ensure the bow does not collapse, push a small roll of tissue paper through the loops of the bow for support and leave to dry. Finally, glue a bow to the top of each pair of tails.

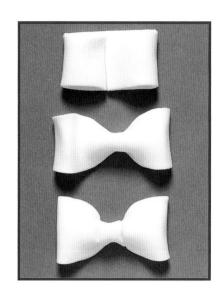

# Ballerinas' Legs

Mix 240g of White Sugar Dough with a little Peach Sugar Dough to make all the flesh parts. Take 15g of the flesh coloured paste and divide in half to make the legs, then roll each piece into a sausage shape 9cm long. Narrow at the ankle and just above and below the knee to make the legs look shapely. Make a diagonal cut at one end to fit on top of the shoe.

At this stage, colour all the paste required for each ballerina's dress, shoes and hair bow. This ensures that each ballerina is colour co-ordinated. For the turquoise ballerina, add SK Gentian Paste Food Colour to White Sugar Dough. For all the other ballerinas, mix the appropriate Sugar Dough colour, i.e. Blue, Green, Peach, Violet, or Yellow, with White Sugar Dough to create pastel shades. You will need 90g of Sugar Dough for each ballerina.

# Ballet Shoes

Make a small sausage shape for each shoe and attach the foot on top using SK Edible Glue. Make the ribbons by rolling a thin lace and criss-cross over the leg, then secure with SK Edible Glue. Repeat this for all the legs in the relevant colours, arranging them into different positions.

# Ballet Skirts

1. Roll out just over 30g very thinly for each layer and cut out with a Garrett frill cutter. Using a PME bulbous cone modelling tool, thin the edges of each curve by rolling out in a rocking motion. Then, using the opposite end of the tool, lift each alternate curve up to accentuate the frill, as shown.

2. Arrange the frill in a circle over the legs on top of the cake. Make three frills for each ballerina and secure in the centre with SK Edible Glue. Lift the edges of the frill and support with foam if necessary until dry. It is useful to position all the skirts before adding the bodice on top of each one.

# Ballerinas' Bodies

1. Make each lower bodice by rolling 10g of the required pastel shade Sugar Dough (as previously described) into a cone shape, pinching gently at the corners.

2. Take the same amount of flesh coloured Sugar Dough and shape the shoulders, then smooth at the top to make a neck. Stick the shoulders onto the bodice using a touch of SK Edible Glue and attach this to the centre of the skirt.

3. Push a stick of dry spaghetti down through the neck and bodice to provide support, leaving some protruding from the top.

4. Finally, roll out a thin strip of coloured paste to go all around the body to hide the join, as shown.

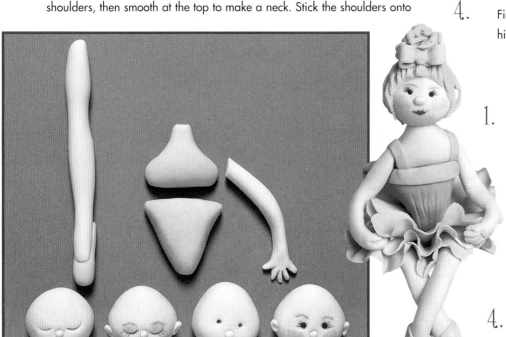

# Ballerinas' Arms

1. For the arms, split just under 10g of the flesh coloured Sugar Dough into equal pieces. Roll one piece into a sausage shape 6cm long. Narrow at the wrist to create a hand, then press it down to flatten slightly.

2. Cut out the thumb and fingers and model the hand. Bend the arm halfway up to make the elbow and pinch at the back to shape it.

3. Glue the arm into position, pressing the shoulder firmly. Make the opposite arm in the same way and attach in place.

4. Cut thin strips of the relevant coloured Sugar Dough to make shoulder straps and attach in place over the join. Decorate as required: I have used little flowers on some.

# Ballerinas' Heads and Faces

1. For the head roll 15g of flesh coloured paste into a very smooth ball. Gently push down over the dry spaghetti and secure with SK Edible Glue.

2. Add the facial features, making some of the ballerinas' eyes shut. Where this is the case, add a light dusting of SK Snowflake Metallic Lustre to the eyelids.

3. Make a tiny rounded cone shape for the nose from the flesh coloured Sugar Dough and glue the pointed end into the hole.

4. Attach two tiny teardrop shapes of flesh coloured paste for the ears.

5. Blush the cheeks and paint the lips with watered down SK Poinsettia Paste Food Colour.

# Ballerinas' Hair

Use a variety of colours for the hair. Fill a sugar shaper with softened Sugar Dough so that it will extrude easily, cover the head with SK Edible Glue and layer the hair. Add a bun or curls and decorate with ribbons or flowers. Enjoy giving each ballerina a personal touch by making slight changes to the basic costumes and hairstyles.

## Materials

20.5cm (8") square cake

Sugar Dough in following amounts:

115g (4oz) Black

135g (4³/₄oz) Brown

50g (1¹/₂oz) Green

8g (¹/₄oz) Peach

25g (just under 1oz) Red

2.5kg (5lb 8oz) White

8g (¹/₄oz) Yellow

SK Paste Food Colours: Berberis, Blackberry, Cactus, Chestnut, Dark Forest, Fuchsia, Holly Ivy, Hyacinth, Leaf Green, Olive, Sunflower, Teddy Bear Brown and Yucca

SK Dust Food Colours: Edelweiss, Purple Mood

SK Edible Gold Paint

SK Edible Glue

Raw spaghetti

## Equipment

35.5cm (14") petal shaped cake drum

Non-stick board

Large and small rolling pins

Sharp knife

PME modelling tool: scallop and comb tool

Sugar shaper

Cutting wheel

Small round cutter

Daisy cutter

Ivy cutter

Leaf cutter and veiner

Medium and fine paintbrushes

Plastic straw

Nail scissors

Florist wire

Cocktail stick

Dark green ribbon to trim

**IMPORTANT** Some of the decorations on this cake contain wires. Ensure these are all removed before the cake is eaten.

# Serendipity in the Wild

This peaceful scene just goes to show that even the wildest of creatures needs a relaxing break from the hustle bustle of the jungle!

In order to make the decoration instructions easier to follow, I have described how to decorate each side of the cake and board individually.

## Covering the Cake and Board

1. To cover the board, take 550g of White Sugar Dough and colour it with SK Olive Paste Food Colour. Once you have covered the board, trim off any excess paste and set aside.

2. To cover the cake you will need 800g of White Sugar Dough. Divide the paste into four 200g pieces and colour each piece using one of the following SK colours: Holly Ivy, Leaf Green, Berberis and Chestnut. Once you have all four colours, randomly mix them together to create a camouflage effect. Roll out and cover the cake, then position the cake in the centre of the covered drum.

## Lion on the Rock

1. For the rock, take 115g of White Sugar Dough and mix with 35g of Black Sugar Dough to make a marbled effect. Take off 110g and set the rest aside.

2. To create a rough surface for the rock, break the paste into three pieces. Place the pieces in a group (with the rough side out) in the centre of the cake. Flatten the paste slightly on the top.

3. Colour 70g of White Sugar Dough with a hint of SK Teddy Bear Brown Paste Food Colour, making

a light brown shade. Cut off 30g for the body and roll into a fat cone shape. Place this on top of the rock.

4. Take off 10g for the back paw and roll into a cone shape 5cm long. Bend in the centre and secure to the body using SK Edible Glue. Mark the paws with the back of a knife. For the front paws, cut off 15g of the paste. Roll half of this into a cone shape for the front leg and paw and make paw marks as before. Roll a small ball for the second paw and mark in the same way, then secure both pieces with SK Edible Glue. Use the remaining paste for the tail and roll into a thin sausage shape. Secure to the back of the lion.

5. Make the head using 15g of the light brown Sugar Dough rolled into an oval shape. Place on top of the body and mark the centre front with the back of a knife. Using a PME scallop modelling tool, indent a smile mark at the bottom end of the line on each side. Add a small beard under the chin using White Sugar Dough. Push the end of a paintbrush into the mouth area and pull down slightly. Use the serrated comb edge of the same modelling

tool to mark the whiskers. Make the eyes from small balls of White Sugar Dough, then add two small black pupils, as shown.

6. To make the mane, colour 30g of White Sugar Dough with SK Chestnut Paste Food Colour. Slightly soften with white vegetable fat, then place in a sugar shaper with a fine hole disc. Extrude lengths of hair and layer on top of the head, starting at the side and working around to the back of the head, finishing at the top. Add the hairs on the end of the tail.

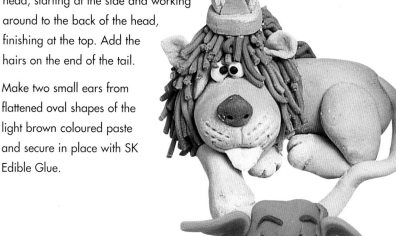

7. Make two small ears from flattened oval shapes of the light brown coloured paste and secure in place with SK Edible Glue.

## Crown

Using a little of the leftover paste, roll out and cut out the crown using the template (page 109). Carefully bend the paste round and glue the ends together. Cut out another thin strip and glue this around the base of the crown. Paint with SK Edible Gold Paint, allow to dry, then fix to the top of the lion's head.

## Rocks and Flower

1. To make the rocks on the board beside the monkey, use the remaining 40g of grey paste left over from the lion's rock. Arrange three rocks on the left hand corner of one side of the cake.

2. Make some foliage from any pieces of Sugar Dough left over from the board and cake. Cut out four leaves using a leaf cutter and vein them in a veiner. Add some SK Cactus Paste Food Colour to some of the paste and roll small cigar shapes, then flatten and mark down the centre with a knife. Using a

sugar shaper, extrude some short lengths of a mixture of green colours and position in the centre.

3. To make the flower, colour 8g of White Sugar Dough with SK Fuchsia Paste Food Colour. Using half of the paste, cut out a number of small daisy shapes. Roll a cocktail stick over each petal to broaden them, then secure to the foliage. Finally, add a flower centre made from White Sugar Dough coloured with SK Sunflower.

## Bananas

1. Take 8g of White Sugar Dough and colour with SK Sunflower Paste Food Colour. Divide equally to make two bananas. Roll each piece into a cigar shape, then cut down the top half of the banana skin to make three equal strips. Dot the outside with SK Chestnut Paste Food Colour using a fine paintbrush.

2. For the banana itself, make a small cone shape from the flesh coloured Sugar Dough and attach in the centre of the banana skin.

# Monkeys

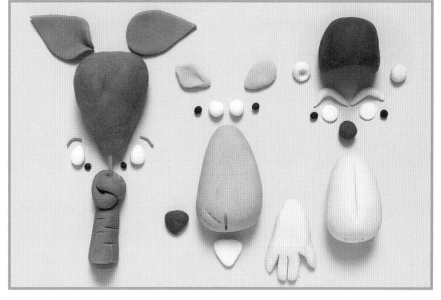

1. For the two monkeys you will need 85g of Brown Sugar Dough and 35g of flesh coloured Sugar Dough. Make the body of one of the monkeys from 30g of Brown Sugar Dough rolled into a cone shape.

2. Mark the chest with the edge of a round cutter. Push a short piece of dry spaghetti into the top to support the head. Make two back legs from 20g of Brown Sugar Dough. Divide the paste in half, roll each piece into a cone shape and fix to the body, bending at the knees. Make two feet in flesh as shown and secure to the legs.

3. Divide 35g equally in two and make cone shapes for the arms. Make the hands from flesh paste then wrap one hand around the banana before securing to the arm. Support the arm holding the banana with foam until set.

4. Make a small leaf shape from Brown Sugar Dough and mark with the back of a knife. Secure in place over the top of the arm to resemble extra hair.

5. Roll 12g of Brown Sugar Dough into a ball to form the top of the head. Using a small circle cutter, take out a section of paste.

6. Roll 15g of flesh coloured Sugar Dough into an oval shape. Glue this inside the cut-out section at the top of the head using SK Edible Glue.

7. Roll two White Sugar Dough balls for the eyes and position them close together in the centre of the face, then add two tiny black pupils. Make two thin curved cigar shapes from Brown Sugar Dough for the eyebrows. Add a small round brown nose. Make two flesh coloured ears, glue to the side of the head and push the end of a paintbrush inside.

8. Repeat this method for the second monkey, adjusting its sitting position, then place one monkey on top of the cake and one near the rocks. Secure with SK Edible Glue.

# "No Diving" Sign

Roll out some Yellow Sugar Dough and cut out a large ivy leaf shape. Using diluted SK Blackberry Paste Food Colour, paint the "No Diving" notice.

# Water

Colour 60g of White Sugar Dough with SK Hyacinth Paste Food Colour. Take off 25g and set the remainder aside. Roll out the paste into an irregular shape for the small pool and secure to the board.

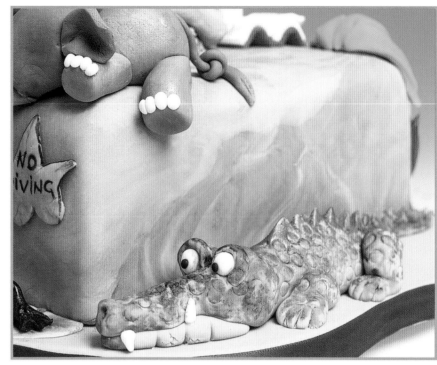

# Palm Tree and Bird

1.  Colour 75g of White Sugar Dough with SK Teddy Bear Brown Paste Food Colour to make a cream colour. Take off 40g for the tree trunk and use the rest to make the leaves. Make a cone shape 10cm long, flatten slightly and curve to make the trunk. Glue the base 1.5cm from the side of the cake and lean the end over to touch the top of the cake.

2.  To make the leaves, cut out several oval shapes. Cut out the edges using the pointed end of a leaf cutter. Arrange the leaves over the side of the cake and around the top of the tree. Paint the markings on the tree using diluted SK Teddy Bear Brown Paste Food Colour and paint the leaves with diluted SK Dark Forest.

3.  Make the bird as described in "Grandma's Garden" (pages 42-49) using oddments of colours to give an exotic look.

# Spiky Foliage

Colour 45g of White Sugar Dough with SK Yucca Paste Food Colour. Take off 18g and set the rest aside. Roll out a strip 10cm x 5cm, take a sharp knife and cut out 'V' shapes until you have seven spikes. Mark the centre of each spike with the back of a knife. Roll up the length of Sugar Dough and allow the spikes to fall naturally, then fix into place behind the tree. Take off 10g and make a smaller one. Fix this to the edge of the pool.

# Diving Bird

1.  Roll 15g of Red Sugar Dough into a cone shape. Cut off at the wide end to make a straight edge. Using a small round cutter, indent two semi-circles into the tail. Position on top of the water, securing with SK Edible Glue.

2.  Take two small pieces of Black Sugar Dough and roll each one into a cigar shape for the legs. Flatten at the end and cut out the webbed feet using a PME scallop modelling tool. Mark the webbed pattern with the back of a knife. Fix to the body and bend over.

# Elephants

1. For both elephants you will need 250g of White Sugar Dough mixed with 50g of Black to make a grey colour. Use 160g for the standing elephant and 120g for the smaller one.

2. For the standing elephant, roll 80g into ball, then make two cuts into the bottom to form the legs using a sharp knife. Gently pull out, narrow very slightly at the top and round off until you have the desired shape for the body. Sit the elephant at the base of the tree. Push a small piece of dry spaghetti into the top of the body to support the head.

3. For the front legs, roll 20g into a sausage shape measuring 9cm, make a diagonal cut 5cm along and make a straight cut at each end. The longer leg is to be on the outside of the elephant and the shorter one on the inside. Fix in place with SK Edible Glue. Make four small toenails from White Sugar Dough and glue around the edges of each foot. Glue the legs to the body.

4. Roll 45g of the grey Sugar Dough into a ball for the head, place the ball down on the work surface and gently roll out the trunk. Pinch out the end of the trunk and push the end of a paintbrush into the tip. Mould a bump on the top of the head. Mark the mouth with small circle cutter and hollow out with a soft paintbrush, pulling the bottom lip downwards. Mark the creases on the trunk with the back of a knife. Roll two small balls of White Sugar Dough for the eyes and add two black pupils. Thinly roll the eyebrows and glue into position.

5. Using a small leaf cutter and 8g of the grey Sugar Dough, cut out two ears

and glue to the sides of the head. Using the remaining paste, roll a thin sausage shape for the tail and mark the hairs at the end with a sharp knife. Fix one end to the elephant and the other to the tree trunk.

6. Make the smaller elephant using the same method but put a knot in the trunk and the tail, as shown.

# Crocodile

1. Colour 170g of White Sugar Dough with SK Olive Paste Food Colour. Take off 115g for the body and head and set the remainder aside.

2. Roll the paste into a ball and then into a cigar shape. Continue to mould until you have the required shape, as shown overleaf. Pinch the top all along the back to the end of the tail to make a ridge. Take a pair of small scissors and cut out the points all along, then neaten. Make two large nostrils using the end of a paintbrush. For the jaw take 10g and make an oval shape. Slide this under the snout, then mark with the back of a knife.

3. Make two back legs from 25g of the SK Olive coloured Sugar Dough. Divide the paste in half and roll each piece into a short cigar shape. Flatten at the end for the foot and mark the claws with a knife. Make the two front legs from 15g of the paste divided in half using the same method.

4. Make scale marks all over the crocodile by pressing the end of a plastic straw into the paste.

5. Add two small balls of SK Olive coloured paste where the eyes are to go and flatten with your finger. Put the white eyes on the top, then add two black pupils. Make two lower and two upper teeth in white and secure in place.

6. Paint the top of the crocodile with watered down SK Holly Ivy Paste Food Colour. When dry, dust over the top with SK Purple Mood Dust Food Colour. Fix to the board.

# Palm Trees

1. Take 50g of Brown Sugar Dough, take off 40g to make the palm tree trunks and set the remaining paste aside. Roll a sausage shape 10cm long for each trunk, then make cuts down the trunk with a small pair of scissors. Glue to the board away from the cake, slightly bend and secure to the top of the cake. Hold in position away from the cake with a thin piece of foam until dry.

2. To make the leaves, roll out 50g of Green Sugar Dough and cut out a 10cm diameter circle. Cut the circle in half, then take a sharp knife and cut out four spiky leaves in each half. Arrange the first layer around the tree and the second layer on top of that. Cut out three more spiky leaves to go on the top.

# Water and Spiky Foliage

Use the remaining 45g of SK Hyacinth coloured Sugar Dough and make a shaped pool in the same way as before. Use the remaining 30g or so of SK Cactus coloured Sugar Dough and make the spiky foliage as before. Fix to the side of the tree.

# Hippo

1. Mix together 50g of White Sugar Dough with 15g of Black to make grey. Take off 20g for the head, roll into a smooth ball and make a small bump on the top, as shown. Roll 20g into a cone and shape a snout. Cut a straight edge at the narrow end and make two large nostrils with the end of a paintbrush. Glue the snout to the head. Make a lower receding jaw from 8g rolled into a flat oval shape and glue underneath the snout. Make two round ball shapes for the ears and mark with the end of a paintbrush. Make two eyes from small round white balls and fix them close together. Add a black pupil on each eye. Make two square-looking short teeth and fix to the upper lip.

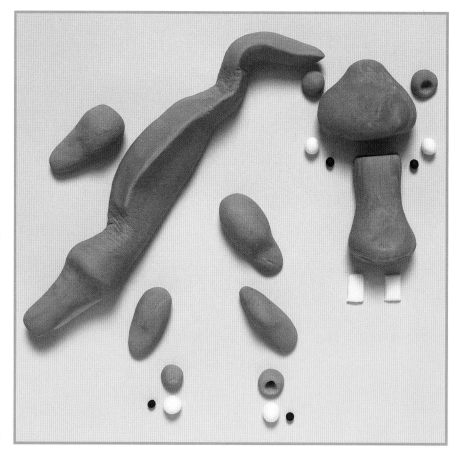

2. For the feet, roll 15g into a short sausage shape, make a diagonal cut at one end and a straight cut at the other. Glue the diagonal end to the water. Add white toenails, as for the elephant.

# Giraffe

1. Colour 200g of White Sugar Dough a warm cream colour with SK Teddy Bear Brown Paste Food Colour. Take off 60g for the body and roll into a fat cone shape. Roll the neck quite thinly until the body is 10cm long. Push a piece of dry spaghetti into the neck and sit this on the side of the cake leaning to one side. Support with foam if necessary.

2. For the legs divide 50g equally and roll into two thin cone shapes. Taper off to create the feet. Use the remaining 10g of Brown Sugar Dough to make two small hooves and glue to the feet. Secure the legs to the side of the body and cross over.

3. Make the front legs from 50g rolled into a sausage shape. Cut diagonally in the centre and glue to the body. Add a hoof to each leg. Take off 30g for the head and make a cone shape, flatten at the front and make two nostrils, add a small teardrop shape for the nose and place on the top. Mark the centre front of the nose with the back of a knife and the mouth with the edge of a small round cutter. Push the end of a paintbrush in the centre of the mouth and make a hole for the straw.

4. Make two small teardrop shapes for the ears and flatten between your finger and thumb. Fix to the sides of the head. Push two short pieces of dry spaghetti into the head for the horns and top with a small ball.

5. Make two small balls from White Sugar Dough for the eyes and add a black pupil in each. Make the eyelids from a small flattened teardrop shape and curve over the top of the eye. Make the tail from a thin sausage shape, then mark the end with a knife.

6. Paint the markings on the giraffe using diluted SK Chestnut Paste Food Colour. Add some black eyelashes to the lids. Dust the stomach area and nose with SK Edelweiss Dust Food Colour.

# Glass of Milk and Book

1. Roll a short sausage shape from 10g of White Sugar Dough. Cut a piece of florist wire long enough to go inside the glass and up into the giraffe's mouth. Add round balls for bubbles on top of the glass. Curve the hoof on the front leg around the glass.

2. To make the book roll out 8g of Red Sugar Dough into a strip measuring 6cm x 2.5cm. Carefully fold over, then open out again, arching the back and front cover. For the pages roll out 20g of White Sugar Dough and cut three strips to measure 5cm x 2.5cm. Lay them one on top of the other and press gently in the centre, then turn up the edge of the top page. Using SK Blackberry Paste Food Colour and a fine paintbrush, paint dots across the pages.

# Ducks Keep Out!

These mischievous ducks are trying their luck in the swans' pond, but without much success!

## Materials

20cm (8") hexagonal cake

SK Sugar Dough in following amounts:

Small amount Black

455g (1lb) Blue

30g (1oz) Brown

185g (6½oz) Green

60g (2oz) Orange

985g (2lb 2½oz) White

290g (10oz) Yellow

SK Paste Food Colours: Chestnut, Holly Ivy, Poinsettia

SK Dust Food Colour: Edelweiss

SK Metallic Lustre Dust Colour: Snowflake

SK Baber Folk Paint: Orange

Squires Kitchen Food Colour Pen: Black

SK Edible Glue

SK Gum Tragacanth

Raw spaghetti

## Equipment

35.5cm (14") round cake drum

Non-stick board

Large and small rolling pins

Sharp knife

PME modelling tools: blade and shell tool, ball tool, serrated cone tool, flower and leaf shaper tool

3 posy pics

Cutting wheel

Small round cutter

Briar rose cutter

Small star cutter

Set of 3 calyx cutters

Medium and fine paintbrushes

Florist wire: no. 24

Fine scissors

Blue ribbon to trim

**IMPORTANT** Some of the decorations on this cake contain wires. Ensure these are all removed before the cake is eaten.

## Covering the Cake and Board

1. Knead together 400g of Blue Sugar Dough and 115g of White Sugar Dough to create a mid-blue shade and cover the board. To create a water ripple effect, press the end of a rolling pin into the paste and gently roll. Once you have the desired effect, trim any excess paste from around the edges with a sharp knife. Remember that the centre area of the board where the cake will be should be left flat.

2. To cover the cake you will need 455g of White Sugar Dough mixed with 60g of Yellow. Knead together the two colours to make a pale lemon shade. Secure the cake in the centre of the board.

## Frieze

1. To make the frieze around the side of the cake, take 60g of Green Sugar Dough and roll out thinly. Cut out three shapes to go around the base of the cake using the template (see page 111).

2. Carefully pick up one of the pieces and turn it over. Brush the back with SK Edible Glue, then attach to the base of the cake, ensuring that the bottom edge abuts the covered cake drum. Carefully brush one of the side edges of the green paste with SK Edible Glue, attach the second piece to the cake and push the pieces together so there is a smooth join. Repeat with the third piece, ensuring that the joins on both sides are smooth.

3. Dilute some SK Holly Ivy Paste Food Colour with a little water. Using a medium paintbrush, stipple around the top of the frieze to create a grassy effect. Allow to dry.

# Pond

To create the pond on top of the cake, take 50g each of White and Blue Sugar Dough. Marble the two colours together, roll out the paste and cut out the pond shape using the template (see page 111). Brush the back of the paste with SK Edible Glue or a little cooled boiled water and attach the pond to the centre of the cake.

# Frog

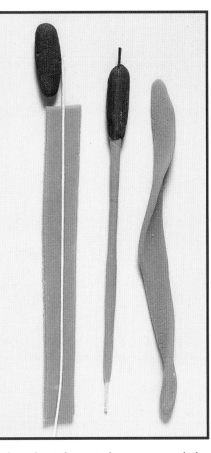

1. Colour 115g Green Sugar Dough a darker shade of green by adding SK Holly Ivy Paste Food Colour. Take off 100g and leave aside. Roll the remaining 15g of dark green Sugar Dough into a cone shape for the frog's body. Round off the wide end to form the head, then push the end of a paintbrush into the front of the head for the eye sockets. Roll two tiny balls of White Sugar Dough and attach into the eye sockets using SK Edible Glue. Draw in the pupils using an SK Black Food Colour Pen. Using the edge of a small round cutter, mark the mouth.

2. Take just under 10g of the dark green paste and divide it in half. Make two sausage shapes, then flatten at one end to create the two back legs. Cut out two 'V' shapes with a knife to form the toes, then fold the legs into position.

3. Make the front legs in the same way but use smaller pieces of Sugar Dough. (They should be about one third of the size.)

# Bulrushes

Cut a 24 gauge wire into 8cm lengths. Roll each piece of wire onto a thin strip of the dark green Sugar Dough to make a slim stem, then top with a small oval made from Brown Sugar Dough. Once you have made enough bulrushes, allow to dry then push a few into each of the posy pics, fill with dark green Sugar Dough and push into the cake. (Alternatively, you can push the bulrushes into a piece of dark green Sugar Dough which can then be attached to the side of the cake, but ensure that the wires do not penetrate the cake.)

# Reeds

1. Take 15g of the dark green Sugar Dough and roll out into a strip. Cut 'V' shapes out of the paste with a sharp knife, smooth the edges with a ball tool and roll up as shown.

2. For the larger reeds, roll slim sausage shapes approximately 5cm long and flatten slightly with a small rolling pin. Arrange as desired on top of the bulrushes.

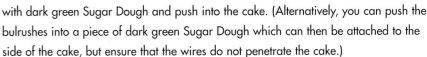

# Water Lilies

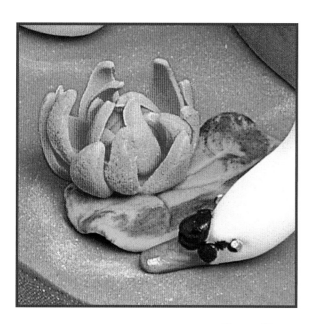

1. You will need 30g of White Sugar Dough for each large water lily. To make the centre, form a small ball of Sugar Dough into a cone. Make a small hook at the end of a piece of 24 gauge florist wire, then dip the hooked end into SK Edible Glue. Slide the cone, wide end facing up, down onto the top of the hook. Press a PME serrated cone tool into the centre of the cone and then, using a sharp craft knife, make equally spaced indentations from the inside of the cone down the side.

2. To make the petals, use three sizes of calyx cutters. Roll out some White Sugar Dough and cut out one set of petals with the smallest cutter, then cut out two sets with the medium cutter and another two with the largest cutter. Thin the petals with a PME ball tool, then cup the petals towards the centre by pushing the ball tool into each petal. Brush water or SK Edible Glue in the centre of each set of petals and slide each one up the wire to the top, starting with the smallest and working up to the largest.

3. Make two pink water lilies in the same way using SK Poinsettia coloured Sugar Dough. Paint the tips of one of the white water lilies with diluted SK Poinsettia Paste Food Colour.

# Lily Pads

Roll out a little Green Sugar Dough and cut out a few lily pads freehand or using a rose petal cutter. Cut out a 'V' shape at the rounded end, then mark the veins with a PME blade tool. Secure onto the cake and board with SK Edible Glue and attach the lilies on top.

# "Keep Out" Sign

Take 30g of White Sugar Dough and roll out thickly. Cut a strip 8cm x 1.25cm, then cut a point at the top. Push a short strand of raw spaghetti into the bottom, leaving some showing to push into the cake. Cut a 2.5cm square for the sign, then write on the message using an SK Black Food Colour Pen. Attach the sign to the post using SK Edible Glue, then push a small piece of dry spaghetti through the notice and into the post for added strength. Paint with diluted SK Chestnut Paste Food Colour. Allow to dry completely, then stand upright and glue to the top of the cake, pushing the spaghetti into the cake for extra support.

# Ducks

1. To make three ducks you will need 230g of Yellow Sugar Dough and 50g of Orange for the feet and beaks. Roll 30g of Yellow Sugar Dough into a cone shape for each body, then continue to shape the thin end for the neck. Push a piece of dry spaghetti down the neck, leaving some showing at the top. Leave to dry before attaching the head.

2. Keeping a nice rounded shape, roll 20g of Yellow Sugar Dough into a cone shape for the head. Position the point at the top of the head, then make an indentation where the beak will fit.

3. Divide just under 10g of Yellow Sugar Dough in half and roll each piece into a bone shape for the cheeks. Flatten both shapes and cut three slits at each end with a sharp knife. Pull the paste out slightly and twist to round off the edges. Glue the cheeks over the indentation in the head.

4. To make the wings, you will need just under 10g of Yellow Sugar Dough for each wing. Follow the method for making the swans' wings below, but just mark the feathers with the back of a knife.

5. Cut out two small star shapes from Yellow Sugar Dough and glue to the top of each duck's head for hair. Arrange the spikes so that the hair looks more natural.

6. Divide just under 10g of Orange Sugar Dough in half for each beak and shape into a triangle. Mark the mouth with the edge of a small round cutter, then secure in place with SK Edible Glue.

7. To make the legs, roll two small sausage shapes of Orange Sugar Dough. Push up at one end, then flatten into a webbed foot and mark with the back of a knife. Make the thighs by rolling two cone shapes from 15g of Yellow

Sugar Dough. Push the end of a paintbrush into the thick end, secure the leg into the hole and glue to the side of the body.

8. Roll two small teardrops of White Sugar Dough for the eyes and attach in place using SK Edible Glue. Add a tiny ball of Black Sugar Dough to each eye for the pupils.

9. When you have made the duck for the top of the cake, make three tiny tears from White Sugar Dough and attach in place down either side of the beak. Glue the ducks into position and support with foam if necessary until dry.

# Swans

1. For the three large swans you will need 215g of White Sugar Dough mixed together with 5ml of SK Gum Tragacanth.

2. For the body, roll 50g of White Sugar Dough into a ball until smooth. Shape this into a cone. The pointed end will be the tail, so lay it down on the work surface and roll the other end into the neck and head, shaping it all in one piece. Fan the tail out a little, then snip the tail feathers with a fine pair of scissors and round off the edges. Split the beak open with a sharp knife. Glue the body of the swan into position on either the cake or board and support the neck with foam until dry.

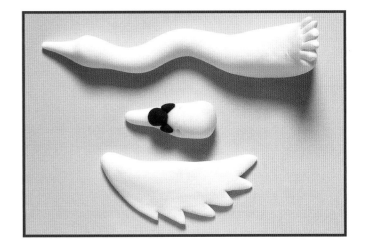

3. Use 15g of White Sugar Dough to make each wing. Roll into an oval shape, then press a rolling pin into the paste halfway down and roll to the edge of the wing to thin it out. Mould into shape, then cut out 'V' shapes with a sharp knife and round off the edges. Glue to the sides of the swan in the desired position and support with foam until dry.

4. Use a small amount of Orange Sugar Dough to make the legs. Secure to the body with SK Edible Glue.

5. Make two more swans in different positions and secure in place with SK Edible Glue.

6. To make the diving swan, use 30g of White Sugar Dough. Roll into a ball then make a point at one end. Mark the tail with the edge of a briar rose cutter. Attach to the board using SK Edible Glue, then make legs in the same way as before and secure in place.

# Finishing Touches

1. Dilute a little SK Holly Ivy Paste Food Colour in a little cooled boiled water and paint the frogs and foliage.

2. Paint the swans' beaks using SK Orange Baber Folk Paint.

3. To make ripples on the water of the cake drum, dust some SK Edelweiss Dust Food Colour over the board using a dry, medium paintbrush. Add a shimmer to the water by dusting with SK Snowflake Metallic Lustre Dust.

## Materials

20cm (8") square cake

Squires Kitchen Sugar Dough in following amounts:

380g (13$\frac{1}{4}$oz) Black

50g (1$\frac{3}{4}$oz) Brown

50g (1$\frac{3}{4}$oz) Green

30g (1oz) Orange

30g (1oz) Peach

1.1kg (2lb 7oz) Red

105g (3$\frac{3}{4}$oz) Violet

1.22kg (2lb 11oz) White

Squires Kitchen Paste Food Colours: Gentian, Holly Ivy, Marigold, Olive, Poinsettia and Teddy Bear Brown

Squires Kitchen Edible Glue

Raw spaghetti

## Equipment

35cm (14") square cake drum

Non-stick board

Large and small rolling pins

Small sharp knife

PME modelling tools: scallop and comb tool, serrated and tapered cone tool, flower and leaf shaper

Sugar shaper

Cutting wheel

7cm (2$\frac{3}{4}$") round cutter

Small holly leaf cutter

Set of PME leaf cutters

Medium and fine paintbrushes

Thin card

Olive ribbon to trim

What better subject for a fun festive cake than Santa's Grotto itself. If required, this cake can be personalised by adding a special Christmas message.

## Covering the Cake and Board

1. Cover the board using 700g of White Sugar Dough.

2. Cover the cake using 800g of Red Sugar Dough.

## Stool

1. Colour 145g of White Sugar Dough with SK Olive Paste Food Colour. Take off 35g for the legs. Roll into a sausage shape 10cm long and cut into four equal pieces.

2. Cut a small rectangle of card to measure 6cm x 5cm, then round off the corners with scissors. Using this template, cut out the seat of the stool. Place this on the work surface, then attach a leg to each corner using SK Edible Glue. Allow to dry, then turn the right way up.

3. Take off 45g of the Olive coloured Sugar Dough, roll out and cut a thin strip measuring 34cm x 3cm. Gather to fit around the chair and secure with SK Edible Glue.

4. Take off 60g of Olive coloured Sugar Dough and form an oval shape for the cushion. Narrow it in at the back of the cushion so that the front is wider than the back. Secure to the seat of the stool with SK Edible Glue.

5. Roll a thin sausage of the same paste and edge the top of the frill to neaten the join.

89

# Santa's Boots

1. Take 25g of Brown Sugar Dough and divide in half. Roll each piece into a cigar shape. Bend one end upwards to make an 'L' shape, then round off and shape like a shoe. Flatten the opposite end with your finger, as shown.

2. Colour 8g of White Sugar Dough with SK Teddy Bear Brown Paste Food Colour, roll out and glue a strip around the top of each boot. For the heel, make a small ball and flatten between your fingers. Do the same again for the soles but make them larger, then cut a straight edge on each. Place a small piece of dry spaghetti into the top of the boot to support the leg.

# Santa

1. For the body, roll 50g of Red Sugar Dough into a pear shape. Insert a stick of dry spaghetti into the narrow end and secure to the seat using SK Edible Glue.

2. Make the legs by dividing 30g of Red Sugar Dough in half. Roll each piece into a cone shape. Push the spaghetti in the boot into the widest end of the leg. Secure the legs to the body, bending at the knee and crossing the left foot over the right.

3. Take the remaining Brown Sugar Dough and make the belt by rolling out a strip long enough to go around the body, approximately 1cm wide. Attach in place. Cut a buckle from a small square of Teddy Bear Brown coloured Sugar Dough and take out the centre using a sharp knife. Glue this to the front of the belt.

4. For the arms, divide 15g of Red Sugar Dough in half and roll into two cigar shapes. Make a diagonal cut at one end of each piece and secure the right arm to the body, bringing it forward so that it rests on the top of the leg. Secure the left arm so that it rests on the side of the leg.

5. Make up enough flesh coloured paste to complete all parts using 150g of White Sugar Dough mixed with a little Peach Sugar Dough. Knead in well, then add a tiny amount of SK Poinsettia Paste Food Colour.

6. For Santa's head, take 25g of the flesh coloured Sugar Dough and roll into a smooth ball. Gently slide the head over the dry spaghetti at the neck and secure with SK Edible Glue.

7. Using a strand of raw spaghetti, make a small hole in the centre of the face for the nose. Roll a small cone shape for the nose and insert it into the hole, securing in place with SK Edible Glue. Using the narrowest end of a PME flower and leaf shaper modelling tool, mark the nostrils. Complete the face, incorporating your own facial expressions.

8. Soften 30g of White Sugar Dough with a little white vegetable fat and fill a sugar shaper. Extrude the paste through the disc with the largest holes to create the beard. Arrange as required and secure with SK Edible Glue.

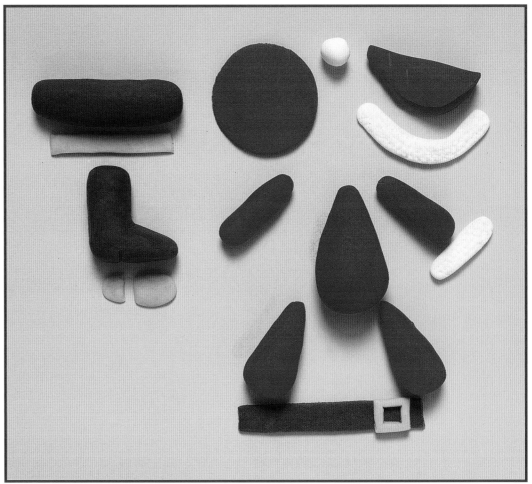

# Santa's Hat

1. Roll out 30g of Red Sugar Dough and cut a circle using a 7cm round cutter. Fold the circle halfway down (see previous page) and place the open end around the front of the head. Secure with SK Edible Glue.

2. Roll 5g of White Sugar Dough into a sausage shape and texture with a PME comb modelling tool. Glue in place around the edge of the hat. Bring the point of the hat to the side and finish off with a ball of White Sugar Dough.

# Little Girl

1. Colour 20g of White Sugar Dough with SK Marigold Paste Food Colour and take off half for the body. Roll into a cylinder and secure to Santa's left leg.

2. Roll a sausage using 8g of White Sugar Dough and cut in half for the legs. Roll two small ovals of Brown Sugar Dough for the shoes and glue to the legs. Roll two thin straps and place these over the join then finish with a small round button. Secure the legs to the body, crossing one leg over the other.

3. Make the frill for the skirt from half of the remaining Marigold coloured Sugar Dough. Cut a strip measuring 10cm x 1.5cm and attach around the body.

4. Roll a small arm and secure to the top of the body, bending at the elbow. Cut a 2cm square of White Sugar Dough and place over the top of the body. Push a short piece of dry spaghetti into the neck to support the head.

5. For the head, roll a small piece of flesh coloured Sugar Dough into a ball and slide over the dry spaghetti. Add the eyes, nose and ears, then mark the smile with a PME scallop modelling tool and blush the cheeks.

6. Fill a sugar shaper with some Brown Sugar Dough softened with white vegetable fat and extrude thin strands for the hair. Finish with an orange bow.

7. For her hand, roll a small ball of flesh coloured paste, mark with the back of a knife and secure in place. Make two hands for Santa and attach in place. Add the white fur trim on his sleeve to finish.

# Santa's Sack

1. Colour 30g of White Sugar Dough with SK Teddy Bear Brown Paste Food Colour. Cut out the base, then roll out and cut out the two sides using the template. Glue the sides of the sack to the base and join at the seams. Mark the creases with a PME flower and leaf shaper modelling tool. Place in position on top of the cake.

2. Make two tall parcels, a candy stick and a lolly from 50g of White Sugar Dough. Add your own decorations using diluted SK Paste Food Colours.

# Back Row Choir

1. Take 35g of Violet Sugar Dough and divide equally for the three bodies. Mould each one into a cone shape with a flat back, measuring 4cm tall. Push a piece of dry spaghetti into the neck of each to support the head.

2. Cut out the shapes for the top of the cassock and the sleeves from thin card. Divide 35g of White Sugar Dough equally into three portions, roll out one piece and cut out the shape for the cassock. Fit the paste around the cone shape, then trim off any excess around the sides, top and neck to create neat edges. Repeat for the other two cassocks.

### Maisie's Handy Hints

Lay the figures flat while you are making and dressing them and allow to dry on a flat board before attaching them to the side of the cake.

3. Make the hands from 8g of flesh coloured paste divided into six. For each hand, make a small sausage 1cm long, slightly flatten at one end and mark the fingers and thumb with a sharp knife. Attach the hands in place with SK Edible Glue. Make small ovals of Brown Sugar Dough for the shoes and secure to the base of the bodies.

4. Place one side of the sleeve over the arm, leaving the hand showing, and bend at the elbow. Glue this on to the shoulder. Repeat with the other arm and for all three choristers, making sure you leave enough room in-between the hands to hold the hymn book. Support with foam if necessary to keep them in position.

5. Take 8g of Violet Sugar Dough and divide equally into three small balls for the collars. Flatten slightly and gently slide over the dry spaghetti around the neck.

6. Make the heads using 25g of flesh coloured Sugar Dough divided into three. Roll into a smooth ball and slip over the spaghetti, then secure with a little SK Edible Glue. Insert the end of a paintbrush into the mouth area and pull down.

7. Add brown or blue eyes to each face and create individual hairstyles for all three choristers using a sugar shaper. I have used Brown Sugar Dough for one and White Sugar Dough coloured with SK Marigold for the others.

8. For the three songbooks you will need a tiny piece of Red Sugar Dough. Cut three strips to measure 3cm x 2cm. Fold loosely in half, making sure the paste does not crack, then mark a spine with the back of a knife. Glue a book to each of the chorister's hands while they are still in a flat position.

9. When dry, glue the choristers to the side of the cake with SK Edible Glue.

# Three Freestanding Choirboys

1. For the three bodies you will need 60g of Violet Sugar Dough divided equally into three. Roll each piece into a cone shape 5cm (2") long. Make a straight cut at the base so that it will stand.

2. Roll six small ovals of Black Sugar Dough for the feet and glue to the base of each cone.

3. Divide 45g of White Sugar Dough into three and make the cassocks in the same way as before. This time, however, they should be slightly bigger.

4. Make the arms and hands from 8g of flesh coloured Sugar Dough as previously described and attach to the body, supporting with foam until dry.

5. Using a tiny piece of Red Sugar Dough, make two more songbooks but this time add a page made from White Sugar Dough over the top before you make the crease. Glue each songbook into position.

6. Make three heads from 25g of flesh coloured Sugar Dough and decorate in the same way as before.

7. Secure one choirboy at the centre back on the cake board and two at the front, as shown.

# Penguins

1. To make nine penguins you will need 360g of Black Sugar Dough, 40g of White, and 25g of Orange.

2. For each body roll 35g of Black Sugar Dough into a cone shape. Pull out a tail at the thickest end and shape the head at the other end. Push a small length of dry spaghetti into the head to support the beak.

3. Mark the eyes with the end of a strand of raw spaghetti and fill with Brown Sugar Dough. Make a small cone shape from Orange Sugar Dough for the beak, mark with the back of a knife and glue to the head. Cut out the feet using a small leaf cutter, make two small 'V' shapes at the front, then glue to the base of each penguin.

4. Make bow ties, scarves and waistcoats from Red and Green Sugar Dough. Attach in place using SK Edible Glue.

5. For the wings, take a small piece of Black Sugar Dough and divide into two equal pieces. Roll two small cigar shapes and flatten slightly. (Remember that if the penguin is dressed, the wings should be secured afterwards.)

6. When you have completed the penguins, position around the cake board and secure with SK Edible Glue.

94

# Ribbons and Decorations

1. Roll out 35g of Red Sugar Dough thinly and cut out long strips for ribbons using a cutting wheel. Thread the ribbon in and around the penguins.

2. For the holly, colour 30g of White Sugar Dough with SK Holly Ivy Paste Food Colour. Roll out and cut out the leaves using a small ivy leaf cutter. Glue three leaves together, then add three small balls of Red Sugar Dough for the berries. Place two of these between the choir singers at the front of the cake and one in each corner of the board. Arrange more leaves around the penguins.

# Baby Reindeer

1. Colour 60g of White Sugar Dough with SK Teddy Bear Brown Paste Food Colour. Take off 30g for the body and roll into an oval shape, then place this onto the board. Push a small piece of dry spaghetti into the front of the body to support the head.

2. For the front legs, roll two small sausage shapes of the same paste. Attach two small balls of Black Sugar Dough for the hooves and mark with the back of a knife. Glue the legs to the front of the body, bringing the hooves together.

3. Roll 15g of the brown paste into a cone shape for the head, then flatten at the nose area. Roll out a tiny piece of paste and cut out two ears with a small leaf cutter. Secure to each side of the head with SK Edible Glue. Roll a small ball of Black Sugar Dough and glue to the nose. Mark two nostrils with a piece of dry spaghetti. Roll two tiny balls of paste for the eyes and flatten, then add a small dot of White Sugar Dough in each.

# Children with Reindeer

1. Make the body and hat for the smaller child from 25g of Red Sugar Dough. Add a head and mark on the facial features. Make the fur trim and mittens from White Sugar Dough and secure with SK Edible Glue. Add black shoes and indent a heel with the back of a knife.

2. Make the other child in the same way using 30g of Green Sugar Dough. Add light brown hair using the small disc on a sugar shaper. Secure in place on the board.

## Materials

20.5cm (8") petal shaped cake

Sugar Dough in following amounts:

30g (1oz) Black

170g (6oz) Green

60g (2oz) Orange

30g (1oz) Peach

15g (1/2oz) Violet

1.55kg (3lb 7oz) White

50g (1³/₄oz) Yellow

60g (2oz) White SK Sugar Florist Paste (SFP)

SK Paste Food Colours: Blackberry, Berberis, Bulrush, Chestnut, Fuchsia, Holly Ivy, Sunflower and Teddy Bear Brown

SK Dust Food Colours: Emerald Isle, Green Envy, Hyacinth, Marigold, Nasturtium, Poppy, Sunflower, Thrift and Violet

SK Metallic Lustre Dust Colours: Brilliant Gold, Copper, Silver

SK Moon Beams Lustre Dust Colours: Jade, Ruby, Topaz

SK Bridal Satin Lustre Dust Colour: Lavender

SK Edible Glue

Clear alcohol or SK Glaze Cleaner

Raw spaghetti

## Equipment

30.5cm (12") petal shaped cake drum

Non-stick board

Large and small rolling pins

Small sharp knife

Craft knife

PME modelling tools: bone tool, scallop and comb tool, serrated and tapered cones tool and flower and leaf shaper tool

Dresden tool

Sugar shaper

Cutting wheel

2cm, 3cm, 4cm and 5cm (³/₄", 1¹/₈", 1¹/₂" and 2") round cutters

Set of 4 PME rose petal cutters

PME blossom plunger cutters

Small and medium calyx cutters

Leaf veiner

Medium and fine paintbrushes

Florist wire: no. 24

CelPad and CelStick

Cocktail stick

Bronze ribbon

# Away with the Fairies

I have never been lucky enough to see fairies at the bottom of the garden, but I'm sure they would be just as enchanting as these fairies! As well as the bright coloured Sugar Dough, I have also used Moon Beams lustre dusts which add a truly magical touch.

## Covering the Cake and Board

Colour 1kg of White Sugar Dough a cream colour using a little SK Berberis Paste Food Colour. Cover both the cake and board, then position the cake centrally on the board.

## Large Toadstool

1. Knead 100g of White Sugar Dough with a small amount of Black Sugar Dough to make a very pale grey shade. Take off 40g and roll into a sausage shape 7cm long. Stand upright and, using the point of a small sharp knife, pluck the surface of the Sugar Dough all the around the centre of the stem and lift away to make a frill, being careful not to cut too deeply. Narrow above and below the frill to shape the stem and widen at the base.

2. Push two lengths of dry spaghetti down into the stem leaving a little showing to support the dome of the toadstool and leave to firm.

**3.** Roll the remaining Sugar Dough into an oval shape for the top. Keeping a rounded shape, place it in the palm of your hand and gently pinch a ridge all around the edge. Using a small sharp knife, make vertical lines all around the top surface.

**4.** Place the dome of the toadstool smooth side down on something that will hold the shape. I have used a 3cm round cutter covered with several layers of cling film, making a cradle. Paint over the vertical lines with diluted SK Bulrush Paste Food Colour and leave the top to dry.

# Foliage, Berries and Flowers

**1.** Mix 40g of Green Sugar Dough with a little SK Holly Ivy Paste Food Colour for the leaves. Roll out the paste and cut out the leaves using the second largest leaf cutter, then use a leaf veiner to texture them. Arrange two layers of leaves around the base of the toadstool and dust with SK Jade Moon Beams.

**2.** Take 15g of Violet Sugar Dough and roll four small balls for the berries, leaving some paste spare. Brush each ball with SK Edible Glue and cover with tiny balls of the same paste. Glue in place around the leaves, then dust with SK Ruby Moon Beams.

**3.** Make four flowers using 4g of White SFP. Take off enough paste to make a small calyx, colour with SK Holly Ivy Paste Food Colour and make a 'Mexican hat' (see Hints and Tips, page 20). Roll out the remaining White SFP very thinly and cut out five flower petals using the smallest rose petal cutter. Thin the edges of each petal by rolling a cocktail stick over the paste, then secure them onto the calyx with SK Edible Glue. Add a small ball of paste for the centre, prick with a cocktail stick and dust with SK Marigold Dust Colour.

**5.** Paint the stem of the toadstool with watered down SK Bulrush Paste Food Colour, using a dabbing motion. Glue the toadstool to the centre of the cake and allow to dry, supporting with foam if necessary. Paint the top with diluted SK Thrift Dust Food Colour, then paint over with diluted SK Topaz Moon Beams.

## Maisie's Handy Hints

Where the cake requires dust colours to be 'painted', mix with clear alcohol or SK Glaze Cleaner and apply with a soft brush. You will have to keep adding the alcohol/glaze cleaner as you work, because it evaporates and dries quickly.

# Large Fairy

**1.** Take 30g of Green Sugar Dough and take off 10g for the body, then divide the remaining paste in half for the legs. Make the body and legs in the usual way. Place the body into the centre of the toadstool and push a stick of dry spaghetti down from the top into the toadstool. Place a leg on either side, crossing over at the knees. Do not attach the arms yet.

**2.** To make the skirt, roll out 15g of Yellow Sugar Dough and, using the third largest rose petal cutter, cut out enough petals for the skirt. Arrange these around the body with the point uppermost. Roll out a tiny piece of Green Sugar Dough cut out the petals to go over the top of the previous row using the smallest rose petal cutter. Attach with the point facing downwards. Dust all the green parts of the fairy with SK Jade Moon Beams.

**3.** To make the wand, cut a 9cm length of no. 24 florist wire. Cut out a small white star using either the template (page 111) or a star cutter, then glue it to the top. Leave to dry, then paint the star with SK Topaz Moon Beams.

**4.** To make the upper body, arms and head, take 15g of flesh coloured Sugar Dough. Take off 4g for the upper body, 4g divided equally into two for the

98

arms and hands, and 8g for the head. Make all the pieces then slide the upper body over the dry spaghetti and secure with SK Edible Glue. Glue the left arm into position with the hand resting on the knee. For the right arm, wrap the fingers around the wand and glue into place.

5.  Decorate the top of the dress using the remaining Yellow Sugar Dough and the smallest rose petal cutter. Slide the head over the dry spaghetti and add the facial features, using diluted SK Bulrush for the eyes and Fuchsia for the mouth.

6.  For the hair, colour 20g of White Sugar Dough with SK Teddy Bear Brown Paste Food Colour to make a pale blonde colour. Soften the paste then place into a sugar shaper with a fine hole disc. Extrude the paste and arrange around the head, securing with SK Edible Glue.

# Fairy's Wings

1.  Colour 35g of White SFP with SK Sunflower Paste Food Colour. For the front set of wings, cut off 15g and roll out very thinly, so that when you hold up the piece, you can see your fingers through it. Cut around the template (page 111) with a craft knife then place the wings on a CelPad and use a bone tool to soften the edges, positioning the ball half on and half off the edge of the paste. Cut a piece of florist wire 3cm long and sandwich it between the wing and a narrow strip of SFP at the bottom inside edge of each wing.

2.  Make the back set of wings in the same way using the template. Remember to place the wire on the front of the wings this time, so that it is not seen from the back.

3.  Decorate both sets of wings by painting SK Green Envy Dust Food Colour on the edges, add dots of SK Copper Metallic Lustre Dust on the top of the large set, then allow the wings to dry in a slightly curved position over a small rolling pin. When dry, paint the back of the wings.

4.  Position the small set of wings by pushing the wire into the back of the toadstool close to the fairy's body. Secure with SK Edible Glue and support with foam if necessary until set. Next, cut four pieces of thin florist wire for the tendrils measuring 10cm. Curl them at the top and push in behind the first set of wings. To neaten at the back, I have added two small green leaves made using the smallest rose petal cutter.

# Orange Fairy

1.  Make a small oval body using 10g of Orange Sugar Dough. Make the legs and feet from 10g of Yellow Sugar Dough then secure to either side of the body and position on the cake. Push a piece of dry spaghetti into the neck to support the head. Make the dress from 30g of Orange Sugar Dough by cutting out three circles using the three largest round cutters. Roll a cocktail stick around the outside edges and carefully indent afterwards to resemble pleats. Cut out the centre of the two largest frills with a 2cm circle cutter and slide over the body. Set the smallest circle to one side and cover with cling film. Arrange and lift the two frills with the end of a paintbrush.

2.  Make the arms from Yellow Sugar Dough, secure in position and push a small length of spaghetti into the end of the right arm to support the hand and wand. Slide the top frill over the spaghetti at the neck.

3. Make the head and hands from 15g of flesh coloured paste.

4. Make the small wand in the same way as the large wand, this time making a star from Yellow Sugar Dough. Curl the fingers of the right hand around the wand and secure with a little SK Edible Glue. Set aside to dry, then push the hand over the spaghetti at the wrist. Continue to support with foam until dry.

5. The frills on the sleeves are made from two small 1.5cm circles cut from Orange Sugar Dough. Frill the edges as before, then fold in half, trim to fit and glue over the wrists.

6. Make the wings from a tiny amount of White SFP using the same technique as for the larger wings (see page 111 for template). Paint all over with SK Sunflower Dust Food Colour then edge and paint the veins with SK Bulrush Dust Food Colour. Finally, stipple SK Poppy Dust Food Colour at the top. Leave to dry over a small rolling pin, then push the ends into the collar of the dress, resting the other end on the cake.

7. For the hair, colour 15g of White Sugar Dough with SK Chestnut Paste Food Colour. Soften the paste and extrude through a sugar shaper. Attach to the head with SK Edible Glue. Take off several strands with a cocktail stick and twist to make curls. Finish with two small flowers made with the smallest blossom cutter.

# Jar of Fairy Dust

Roll 15g of Orange Sugar Dough into an oval shape. Push the end of a paintbrush into the top and widen with your fingers. Roll a small ball for the lid and top with a tiny knob. Paint the jar with SK Thrift Dust Food Colour.

# Acorn Pixie

1. Use 10g of Green Sugar Dough to make the body. Roll into an oval shape and place on the edge of the cake. Push a piece of dry spaghetti into the neck to support the head.

2. For the legs and jacket colour 20g of White Sugar Dough with SK Teddy Bear Brown Paste Food Colour to make a light brown shade. Take off 15g for the legs and divide equally, then roll each into a cone shape measuring 5cm. Push the end of a paintbrush into the thickest end and thin the edges with your fingers. Secure to the body and position as shown in the main picture. Make two small shoes from 4g of Green Sugar Dough, as shown, and push into the trouser. Make the jacket from the remaining brown coloured Sugar Dough, using the template (page 111) as a guide.

3. Take 15g of Green Sugar Dough and divide equally for the arms. Make two shapes as described for the legs and secure into position using SK Edible Glue. Cut four leaves using the smallest leaf cutter, mark with the back of a knife and glue over the jacket. Make the head and hands from 10g of flesh coloured paste.

4. To make the acorn hat, colour 5g of White Sugar Dough with SK Bulrush Paste Food Colour. Roll into a cone shape and cut a straight edge at the widest part. Secure to the head and top with a small Mexican hat shape made from the same colour as the jacket. Extrude some strands of light brown coloured paste from the sugar shaper and curl around the brim.

5. Paint the hair at the back of the head with SK Bulrush Paste Food Colour. Dust the hat and leaves with SK Topaz Moon Beams.

6. Make a jar of Magic Dust as described above, but this time use White Sugar Dough tinted with SK Berberis Paste Food Colour. Secure to the cake and dust around it with SK Marigold Dust Food Colour.

# Ladybird

Make the ladybird, as described in "Grandma's Garden" (pages 42-49).

# Toadstools with Acorns

1. For the base and leaves tint 25g of White Sugar Dough with SK Berberis Paste Food Colour. Take off 5g and roll into a ball, flatten with your fingers into an oval shape and place onto the board. Make a second shape from 8g and place alongside the first. Secure with SK Edible Glue.

2. For the three toadstools, colour 45g of White Sugar Dough with a little Black Sugar Dough to make a pale grey shade. Make small, medium and large toadstools using the following method: roll a sausage shape and cut to the height required; stand the stalk upright and make it thicker at the base; push a piece of dry spaghetti down the centre; roll the top into a cone shape and indent the inside with a tapered cone tool, making it wide enough to fit over the stalk; secure with SK Edible Glue; mark the top using a Dresden tool. Arrange the toadstools on the base.

3. Colour 8g of White Sugar Dough with SK Bulrush Paste Food Colour and make four oval shapes for the acorns. Add a tiny point on the end of each and secure with SK Edible Glue around the largest toadstool.

4. Roll out the remaining Berberis coloured paste, cut out some leaves using the third largest leaf cutter, mark with a veiner or with the back of a knife and secure with SK Edible Glue. Dust with SK Topaz Moon Beams. Add three flowers made from a little Yellow Sugar Dough using the medium blossom plunger.

# Pixie on Toadstool

1. Make a thin 8cm long sausage shape from Green Sugar Dough for the legs. Cut in half and turn up at the end to form a foot. Glue the legs to the top of the medium toadstool. Make a small Mexican hat shape using a tiny piece of Yellow Sugar Dough for the body and position over the top of the legs. Push a small stick of dry spaghetti into the neck to support the head.

2. To make the arms, roll some Green Sugar Dough into a sausage shape 5cm long, cut in half and secure to the body, bending at the elbow.

3. For the head and hands, take a tiny piece of flesh coloured Sugar Dough, make two tiny oval hands, then roll the head and decorate in the usual way, adding two pointed ears. Paint on the hair using diluted SK Chestnut Paste Food Colour. Make a small cone shaped hat and glue to the head.

# Pixies with Book

1. For the yellow pixie, you will need 15g of Yellow Sugar Dough. Make the body from 4g rolled an oval shape and place on the board. Roll 8g into a sausage shape 8cm long, taper both ends to a point and turn up at both ends to form the feet, as shown. Cut into two, make a diagonal cut at the thickest end and secure to the body. Bend at the knee and turn the feet out, then glue the heels together.

2. Make the arms from 4g of Yellow Sugar Dough divided equally. Roll into a sausage shape and bend at the elbow, then secure to the body and board.

3. For the collar and hat, take 4g of

Peach Sugar Dough, roll out thinly and cut a 3cm calyx for the collar. Glue this over the top of the body. Make a Mexican hat shape from Peach Sugar Dough, roll out to widen and thin using a CelStick or cocktail stick, then cut out the shape using a small calyx cutter, as shown.

4. Make the head and hands from 5g of flesh coloured Sugar Dough and secure into position, leaving enough room between the hands for the book. For the hair, extrude a little Chestnut coloured Sugar Dough through the sugar shaper. Place the hat on top and secure with SK Edible Glue.

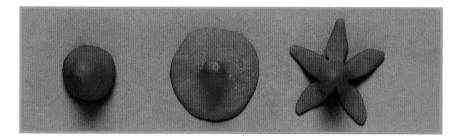

# Kneeling Pixie

1. For the body, shape 4g of White Sugar Dough into a cone. Roll another 4g into a thin sausage and make a diagonal cut in the centre for the legs. Secure one end of the legs to the body and gently bend into a kneeling position. Open the knees slightly, then make two tiny oval shapes for the shoes. Roll a tiny sausage for the arms, secure to the shoulder and bring forward to rest on the leg.

2. Using 4g of flesh coloured Sugar Dough, roll the head into a teardrop shape, add two pointed ears, then paint on the facial features and the hair. Add a collar and hat made from White Sugar Dough, as described for the yellow pixie. Finally, paint the top of the body with SK Green Envy Dust Food Colour, paint the hat, collar and trousers with SK Poppy, and paint the shoes with SK Blackberry. Secure the pixie to the board when complete.

# Toadstools with Frog and Butterfly

1. Colour 25g of Green Sugar Dough with a little SK Holly Ivy Paste Food Colour. Take off 10g for the base and set the rest aside. Shape into a flat oval and indent with your fingers to make it bumpy. Using 5g of the paste, make a small frog as described in "Ducks Keep Out" (pages 84-88).

2. Make the large and small toadstool as before using 30g of White Sugar Dough mixed with a little Black. Position the toadstools and the frog, as shown in the main picture. Roll out the remaining Green Sugar Dough and make some leaves using the third largest leaf cutter. Make two flowers using the large blossom cutter, as shown.

3. Paint the large toadstool with SK Nasturtium Dust Food Colour and the small toadstool with Marigold. Paint the markings on the frog with SK Emerald Isle.

4. Make the butterfly from thinly rolled White Sugar Dough. Cut out the shape using a small butterfly cutter or using the template (page 111) as a guide. Secure the wings to a tiny sausage shape of Black Sugar Dough and leave to dry. Decorate with SK Brilliant Gold Lustre Dust and SK Hyacinth Dust Food Colour. Glue to the top of the large toadstool.

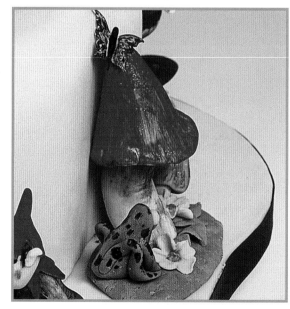

# Bookworm Fairy

1. Make the base from 10g of Green Sugar Dough. Make three flat toadstools from 45g of pale grey Sugar Dough, as previously described. Position on top of the base, then paint the tops with SK Violet Dust Food Colour. Add some grass around the base of the toadstools and three Orange Sugar Dough flowers using the middle size blossom cutter.

2. Roll out 15g of White SFP very thinly and cut out the wings using the template for the large fairy's front set of wings (page 111). Make the wings as previously described, then paint all over with SK Lavender Bridal Satin Lustre Dust. Paint the edge with SK Violet Dust Food Colour. Set aside.

3. This fairy is made in the same style as for the large fairy, with a flesh upper body. Colour 6g of White Sugar Dough with SK Bulrush Paste Food Colour, take off 4g for the lower body and set the rest aside. Shape into a cone with a flat top and place on the toadstool, then insert a piece of dry spaghetti at the neck.

4. For all the flesh parts you will require 8g of flesh coloured paste. Take off half for the upper body and arms and use the other half for the head. Make the upper body and slide over the spaghetti, then make the legs from 8g of White Sugar Dough, as shown. Secure to the body and bend each leg at the knee, bringing the feet to rest on the top of the toadstool. Cover the top of the legs above the knees with a thin piece of SK Bulrush coloured Sugar Dough, wrapping around loosely to resemble a skirt.

5. Make the arms and hands in one piece, resting on the knees ready to hold

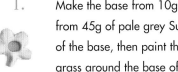

the book. Cut out two small circles from Bulrush coloured Sugar Dough for sleeves to cover the join at the shoulder.

6. Fill the sugar shaper with softened Yellow Sugar Dough, extrude the paste through the fine hole disc and arrange over the head. Make the hat from a hollowed out cone of White Sugar Dough and pull out into two points at the top.

7. Paint the stripes on the hat and legs using SK Poppy Dust Food Colour, then dust all the dress parts with SK Topaz Moon Beams.

8. Glue the wings to the back of the fairy and support with foam if necessary until dry.

# Books

For the two closed books you will need 4g of Peach Sugar Dough and 4g of Orange. Cut out a strip measuring 4cm x 2cm. For the pages, roll out 4g of White Sugar Dough cut a strip measuring 3.5cm x 2cm. Cut this strip in half to make two pages, place one on top of the other and secure on one side of the cover, as shown. Fold the cover over the pages and mark the spine with the back of a knife. Glue to the top of the toadstool. Make a smaller book in the same way as the yellow pixie and glue to the fairy's hands.

# Six Toadstools

Make a base 12cm long from 25g of Green Sugar Dough. To make all the toadstools take 100g of White Sugar Dough tinted with Black and make as previously described. Paint the tops of the first group with SK Bulrush Dust Food Colour. Paint the flat topped ones with SK Poppy Dust Food Colour, then add a few small circles in white to the top

when dry. The last one is painted with SK Nasturtium Dust Food Colour. Add a little grass and blossom flowers. Finally, dab a little SK Bulrush Dust Food Colour to shade around the grass.

## Materials

20.5cm (8") square cake

SK Sugar Dough in following amounts:

90g (3oz) Black

20g (³⁄₄oz) Peach

1.3kg (2lb 14oz) White

SK Paste Food Colours: Berberis, Poinsettia, Rose and Teddy Bear Brown

SK Metallic Lustre Dust Colours: Bronze and Silver

SK Baber Folk Paints: Brown, Red

SK Edible Glue

SK Gildesol

SK Confectioners' Glaze

Raw spaghetti

## Equipment

28cm x 23cm (11" x 9") oval cake drum

Non-stick board

Large and small rolling pins

Taffeta veining rolling pin

Sharp knife

PME modelling tools: scallop and comb tool, serrated and tapered cones tool

Cutting wheel

Design wheel

Garrett frill cutter

10cm, 5cm, 3cm and 2.5cm (4", 2", 1¹⁄₈" and 1") round cutters

Small heart cutter

Small briar rose cutter

Small blossom cutter

Fine and medium paintbrushes

Metal ruler

# Just Married

This wedding cake would make an ideal gift for a bride and groom. You can personalise the design as much as you wish to make it extra special.

## Covering the Cake and Board

1. Cut the cake into two pieces for the suitcases. The easiest way is to cut it in half so that you are left with two 20.5cm x 10cm rectangles. From these pieces, cut one rectangle measuring approximately 15 x 10cm and one measuring 12.5cm x 7.5cm.

2. Roll out 225g of White Sugar Dough and cover the cake drum. Texture the paste with a taffeta rolling pin, then brush with SK Snowflake Metallic Lustre Dust.

3. Colour 700g of White Sugar Dough with a little SK Berberis Paste Food Colour. Roll out and cover the two cakes, tucking the paste underneath the cake for both suitcases. Put the leftover paste to one side.

4. Using a clean metal ruler, press a horizontal line across the front of the suitcases and round the sides. Run a design wheel above and below this line to make stitch marks. Make another line with the ruler just below the lower stitched line, again around the front and sides. Add stitch lines around the top of the small case.

## Large Suitcase Decoration

1. Roll a long, thin sausage of the Berberis coloured paste and attach around the top of the large case with SK Edible Glue.

2. To make the straps for the large suitcase, roll out 20g of the Berberis coloured Sugar Dough and cut out two strips measuring 7.5cm x 1.5cm. Colour 45g of White Sugar Dough with SK Teddy Bear Brown Paste Food Colour. Roll out the paste and cut out two strips slightly larger than the lighter strips. Glue the strips together and round of the ends of each strap, then run stitch marks around the top with a design wheel.

3. Make eyelets for the straps by securing a small ball of Teddy Bear Brown coloured Sugar Dough to the straps, then push the end of a paintbrush into the centre to make a hole.

4. Make a buckle from the same paste for each strap and secure in place. Carefully lift the straps and fix to the cake, taking care as you bend the paste.

5. Roll out some of the Berberis coloured Sugar Dough and cut out a handle for the case. Glue in place and support with a piece of foam until dry.

6. Secure the large case to the board, leaving more room at the front than the back.

Just Married

# Small Suitcase Decoration

1. To make the clasps on the case, cut out two 2cm x 3cm rectangles and one slightly smaller rectangle from the Berberis coloured paste. Make rivet marks in each corner using a PME serrated cone modelling tool. Make a small catch from the same paste.

2. Brush all the pieces with SK Gildesol, ensuring you have a thin, even covering, then use a dry brush to apply SK Bronze Metallic Lustre Dust. Burnish with a soft brush to bring out the colour and shine.

3. Glue the clasps in place - you will only need one on the side where the bride will sit.

4. Make a handle in the same way as for the large case, secure and support until dry. Place the small suitcase on top of the larger one.

## Label

1. Roll out 15g of White Sugar Dough and cut out a rectangle 6cm x 2.5cm. Trim one end to a point and push a hole through using the end of a paintbrush. Cut out a small heart from White Sugar Dough, allow to firm, then attach to the label. Paint with SK Red Baber Folk Paint.

2. Using SK Brown Baber Folk Paint and a fine paintbrush, paint "Just Married" onto the label, or a message of your choice. Allow to dry.

3. Attach the label in place, then roll a thin sausage of White Sugar Dough and carefully thread it through the hole. Twist it around the suitcase handle and secure with SK Edible Glue.

## Groom's Body

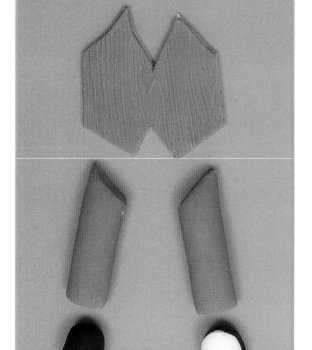

1. Mix 90g of White Sugar Dough with a small amount of Black Sugar Dough to make a pale grey shade. Take off 30g for the body and roll an oval. Place the body on top of the case, then push a piece of raw spaghetti down through the body, leaving some showing at the top.

2. Take another 45g of the grey paste, roll into a sausage shape and cut in two for the legs. Secure to the body and drape over the side of the suitcase. Push a short length of spaghetti into the end of each trouser leg.

3. To make a waistcoat, roll out 15g of the grey paste and cut out a rectangle 6cm x 6cm. Texture the paste with a taffeta rolling pin and, then cut to shape using the template (page 111) as a guide. Fit to the front of the body.

4. Make the spats from two small rounds of White Sugar Dough. To make the shoes, divide 10g in two and roll two ovals. Glue the spats to the front of each shoe, then apply a dab of glue to the end of each leg and slide the shoes onto the spaghetti. Support with foam until dry.

5. To finish the legs, cut out two strips of grey paste for the turn-ups and glue into place.

## Tail Coat

1. Roll out 30g of Black Sugar Dough and cut out the shape for the tail coat (page 111). Glue to the body, leaving an opening at the front to show the waistcoat. Arrange the tails over the back of the suitcase and glue into place.

2. Take a tiny piece of Black Sugar Dough and make the lapels using the template (page 111). Texture with the taffeta rolling pin and secure in place with SK Edible Glue.

## Groom's Head

Roll a ball from 30g of flesh coloured Sugar Dough and slide over the spaghetti at the neck. Add all the facial features, creating the smile using either a scallop modelling tool or a small round cutter. Paint on the hair using diluted SK Brown Baber Folk Paint.

## Collar

Take 5g of White Sugar Dough and cut a rectangle 5cm x 1cm. Make a cut in the centre of the paste, then glue the strip under the chin and around the neck.

## Cravat

Colour 40g of White Sugar Dough a pale pink shade using SK Rose Paste Food Colour. Take off 5g for the cravat, cut into a thin strip and form a tie shape. Add a small knot and secure in place.

## Carnation

Roll out a very thin strip of the Rose coloured Sugar Dough measuring 2.5cm x 1cm and cut out a fringe using a sharpe knife. Curl the strip from one side to the other in a flower shape, then glue to the lapel.

## Top Hat

Roll out 30g of Black Sugar Dough and cut out a 5cm diameter circle for the brim. Cut a circle with a 2.5cm round cutter from the centre of this circle for the top. For the sides of the hat, roll out a strip 2.5cm wide and 8cm long and glue this around the outside of the circle, joining neatly at the back. Secure the brim to the bottom, then add a strip of grey paste for the hat band. When complete, secure to the groom's head. Brush the hat band with SK Silver Metallic Lustre Dust.

## Bride

1. Make the upper body of the bride and push a piece of spaghetti into the neck. Allow to dry for a few hours so that the paste is firm enough to support the head.

2. To make the legs, roll 20g of flesh coloured Sugar Dough into a slim sausage shape approximately 21cm long. Cut in half and make a diagonal cut at the ankle.

3. Make two ballet shoes from 5g of the Rose coloured Sugar Dough and secure onto the legs. Glue the legs into position, leaving room in-between for the body.

4. To make the petticoat, roll out 25g of the Rose coloured paste and cut out a Garrett frill shape. Gently roll a cocktail stick over each scallop to frill the

paste. Cut the frill, then arrange in a circle over the legs. Make another frill if required, then add a white frill on the top.

5. Roll out 30g of White Sugar Dough and texture with the taffeta rolling pin. Cut out a 10cm circle and place over the petticoat.

6. To make the body, roll 20g of White Sugar Dough into a pear shape then mould to the shape of the body. Push a spaghetti strand into the top, then secure in the centre of the skirt. Push the upper body over the spaghetti and secure.

7. Make the arms from 10g of flesh coloured paste: they should each be 8cm long.

8. Roll out a little White Sugar Dough very thinly and cut out a number of circles using a small briar rose cutter. Shape into petals, then attach so that they overlap around the bodice. Make two slightly larger circles for the sleeves and secure in place so that the join at the shoulder is covered.

9. Make the head and paint on the face, adding two small balls of White Sugar Dough for the earrings. If necessary, support the back of the body with foam while you are doing this.

10. For the hair, roll a ball of flesh Sugar Dough and push in the centre with the end of a paintbrush to create a bun. Secure to the top of the head, then paint on the hair with diluted SK Brown Baber Folk Paint and a fine paintbrush.

# Groom's Arms

1. Make the groom's arms from a sausage of Black Sugar Dough, then make a diagonal cut at the shoulder. Take 5g of flesh coloured Sugar Dough and divide in two. Make the left hand and secure to the left arm, then attach the complete arm in place on the bride's skirt.

2. Make the right hand, ensuring the fingers are long enough to hold the glass and attach to the right arm.

# Champagne Glass

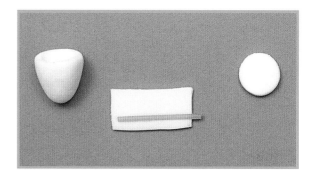

1. Take a tiny piece of White Sugar Dough and roll it into a ball. Push the paste over the end of a tapered cone tool to create a hollow. Cut out a small circle for the base. For the stem, roll a tiny piece of paste around a short piece of raw spaghetti, then push the end of the stem into the glass, securing with SK Edible Glue. Allow all the pieces to dry, then attach the base to the stem and allow to dry, supporting with foam if necessary.

2. Secure the glass to the groom's right hand, then attach the arm in place. Support with foam until dry.

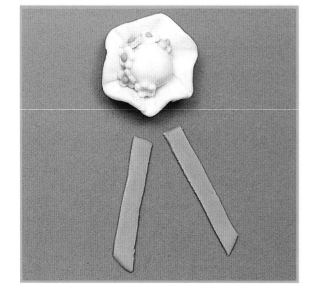

# Veil

1. Thinly roll out 15g of White Sugar Dough to the shape of the veil. Gather with the end of a paintbrush to create gentle pleats, then gather at the top and cut out a crescent shape with a small round cutter to fit around the bun. Secure with SK Edible Glue and arrange down the back of the bride.

2. Make several tiny roses and arrange around the head.

# Bouquet

1. Cut out and frill a 3cm circle of White Sugar Dough. Leave to dry resting on top of a small round cutter and drop a small ball of paste in the centre.

2. Once dry, cut out a number of flowers with the smallest blossom cutter and arrange over the ball of paste.

3. Make two trailing ribbons from Rose coloured Sugar Dough and glue in place. Attach the bouquet in place.

# Rose Petals

As a finishing touch, make a few rose petals from thinly rolled Rose and White Sugar Dough using a rose petal cutter. Scatter around the board and secure with SK Edible Glue.

# Finishing Touches

Brush SK Confectioners' Glaze over the groom's top hat, lapels, shoes and over the bride's hair to add a shine to the finished piece.

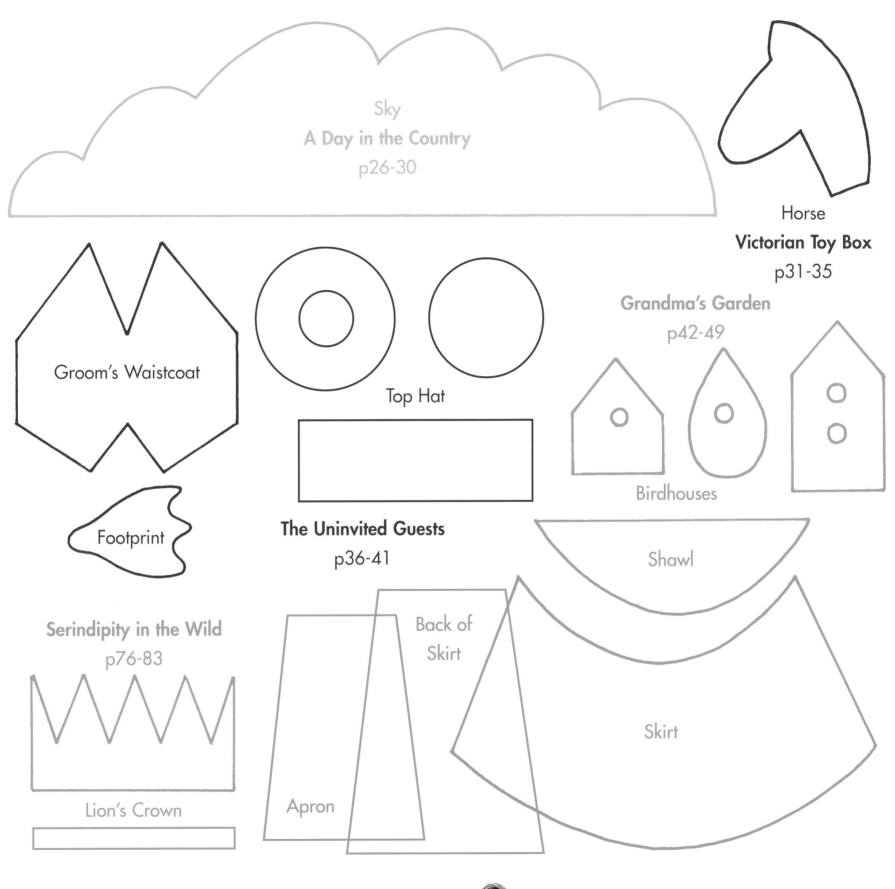

Sky
**A Day in the Country**
p26-30

Horse
**Victorian Toy Box**
p31-35

Groom's Waistcoat

Top Hat

Grandma's Garden
p42-49

Footprint

**The Uninvited Guests**
p36-41

Birdhouses

Shawl

**Serindipity in the Wild**
p76-83

Back of Skirt

Skirt

Lion's Crown

Apron

Side (x2)

Back

Front

**Piggy Plonk** p58-62 Wheelbarrow

Base

Handle

Wheel Support

Wheel

Boat Base

Bow Tail

**Dance Ballerina, Dance!**
p72-75

Bogey Creek

Camper's Pool

**Gone Fishin'**
p63-71

Green Tree

Green Tree

Brown Tree

Boat Side (x2)

Frieze

Boat Back

Jetty Side (x2)

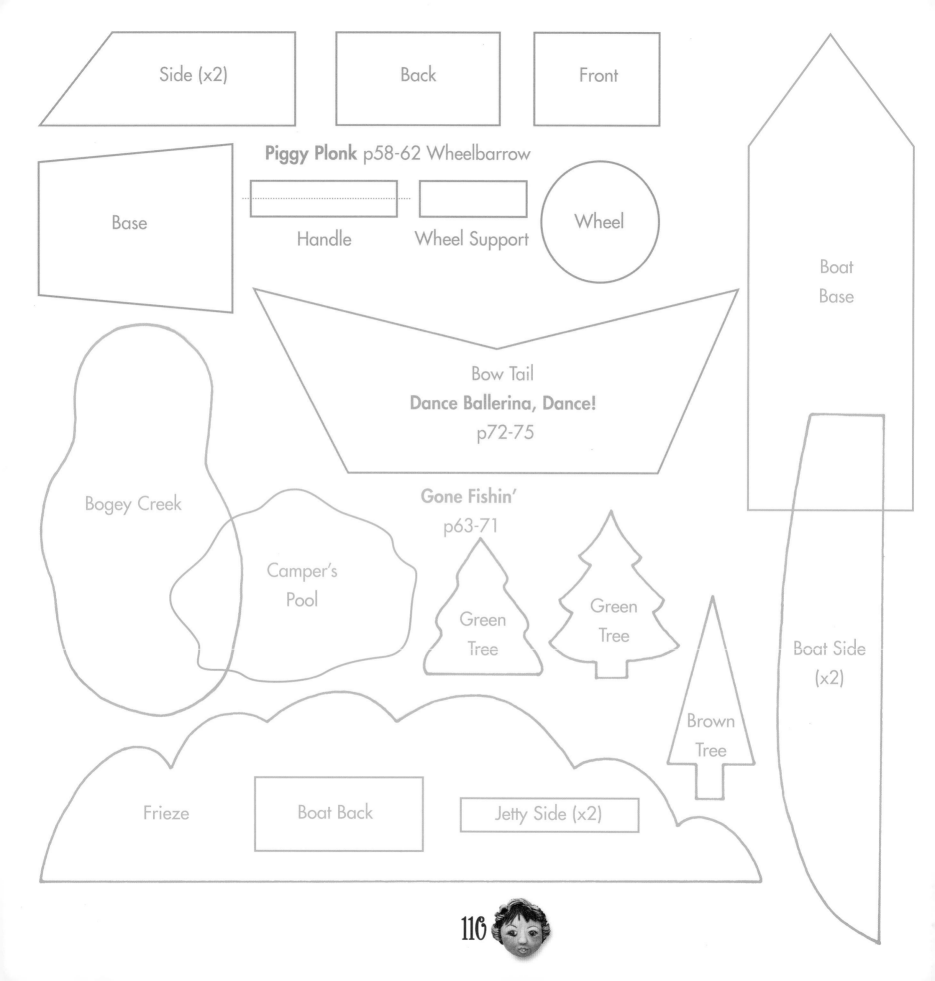

Wand Star

Large
Fairy
Wing
(Front)
(x2)

Large
Fairy
Wing
(Back)
(x2)

Orange
Fairy Wing
(x2)

Acorn Pixie
Jacket

Butterfly

Just Married
p104-108

Groom's Tailcoat

Lapel
(x2)

Away with the Fairies
p96-103

Pond

**Ducks Keep Out**
p84-88

Groom's Waistcoat

Frieze

# Stockists

## Manufacturers and Distributors

**Cakeboards**
George Street
Burnley
Lancashire
BB11 1LX
Tel: 01282 423142
E-mail: info@cakeboards.co.uk
Manufacturer of cake boards, cake decorations and specialist printed bakery papers.

**Culpitt Cake Art**
Jubilee Industrial Estate
Ashington
Northumberland
NE63 8UQ
Tel: 01670 814545
Web site: www.culpitt.com
Manufacturers and wholesale suppliers of cake decorating and sugarcraft equipment and decorations.

**FMM**
Unit 5
Kings Park Industrial Estate
Primrose Hill
Kings Langley
Hertfordshire
WD4 8ST
Tel: 01923 268699
Manufacturers and suppliers of cake artistry, bakery and catering equipment.

**Guy, Paul & Co.**
Unit B4, Foundry Way
Little End Road
Eaton Socon
Cambridgeshire
PE19 3JH
Tel: 01480 472545
Web site: www.guypaul.co.uk
Trade suppliers of tools and materials for the art of bakery, sugarcraft and food decoration.

**Holly Products**
Holly Cottage
Hassall Green
Sandbach
Cheshire
CW11 4YA
Tel: 01270 761403
Suppliers of moulds, embossers, patterns and tools via mail order.

**PME Sugarcraft**
Brember Road
South Harrow
HA2 8UN
Tel: 020 8864 0888
Manufacturers of sugarcraft tools and cutters.

**Squires Group**
Tel: +44 (0)1252 711749
Web site: www.squires-group.co.uk
Online shop: www.squires-shop.com
Manufacturer of Sugar Dough.

## Shops

**Almond Art**
Units 15-16
Faraday Close
Dorse Lane Industrial Estate
Clacton-on-Sea
Essex
CO15 4TR
Tel: 01255 223322
Mail order and show room.

**Jane Asher Party Cakes and Tearoom**
22-24 Cale Street
London
SW3 3QU
Tel: 020 7584 6177
Web site: www.janeasher.co.uk
Producer of handcrafted couture cakes, supplier of baking, decorating and sugarcraft equipment. Shop, tearoom and mail order.

**Confectionery Supplies**
Unit 11
Foley Trading Estate
Hereford
HR1 2SF
Tel: 01432 371451
Shop, school and trade supplier.

**Corteil & Barratt**
40 High Street
Ewell Village
Surrey
KT17 1RW
Tel: 020 8393 0032
Shop and school.

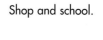

**Orchard Products**
51 Hallyburton Road
Hove
East Sussex
BN3 7GP
Tel: 01273 419418
Manufacturers and suppliers of fine quality sugarcraft cutters and tools. Shop and mail order.

**Squires Kitchen Sugarcraft**
(International School of Cake Decorating and Sugarcraft)
Squires House
3 Waverley Lane
Farnham
Surrey
GU9 8BB
Tel: 01252 711749
Web site: www.squires-group.co.uk
Online shop: www.squires-shop.com
Sugarcraft colours, tools, equipment, Sugar Dough, marzipans and sugarpastes. Shop, school and mail order.

## Publications

**Squires Kitchen Magazine Publishing Ltd.**
Alfred House
Hones Business Park
Farnham
Surrey
GU9 8BB
Tel: 01252 727572
Web site: www.squires-group.co.uk
Publishers of Cakes & Sugarcraft Magazine, Wedding Cakes - A Design Source, Wedding Dresses - A Design Source and Christmas Cakes, Desserts and Sweets.